YOUR BLACK DIARY

BECOME INVINCIBLE SECRETLY IN THE GAME OF LIFE

KRISHNA YOGA

To Generation Alpha,

Don’t be scared, explore deeply.

Contents

Preface

At 11 years old, he sat there in a corner, quietly! With tears in his eyes and silence on his face, he did not move. He was confused and had no direction on how to proceed in life at this young age. Negativity surrounded him as if it was his natural habitat. At that moment, his mom walked in and saw him. She asked what was wrong, and he silently shook his head "no." With a heart full of compassion, she hugged her son tightly and told him the secrets of a happy life and that everything would be alright.

He listened to her words with skepticism but ultimately decided to give it a try. And over the next several years, he emerged as an accomplished young man - despite all the challenges life had thrown at him! He made new friends, overcame obstacles, and got into pretty tight spots. But through it all, he never lost sight of what his mom had told him back in that corner: That everything would be alright. And eventually, it was.

Practically speaking, not all parents have the time to impart their life learnings to their children in this fast-moving world. Children are on their own trying to figure out how to navigate. This thought shook me and made me think of the fate of the upcoming generations. I see the need to explain the "secrets of a happy life" to every child in the simplest of words and provide them with directions and practice sheets to put these theories into play.

I decided to retire from my corporate position and now live in the Himalayas to devote my time to this noble cause. And so, I am now publishing a book titled "your BLACK DIARY."

The guiding philosophy behind the book is that everyone can be happy and has the potential to flourish - no matter what life throws their way. It's all about finding our passion in life and pursuing it relentlessly with enthusiasm. Once we've found that thing that makes us happy, everything else falls into place - irrespective of how challenging or frustrating our circumstances may be at any given moment!

Introduction

We have come a long way. Isn't it? We have actively been part of the evolution that unfolds even today. The biological evolution of living things is what we think of when we use the word "evolution." But there are other sorts of "evolution" as well, including the mechanisms through which the universe, stars, galaxies, and planets originate and evolve. Even though the processes involved are very diverse, there is change over time in each of these situations. The word evolution also applies to our religious beliefs. We have seen the age of Judaism, Christianity, Islam, Zoroastrianism, Baha'i, Hinduism, Buddhism, Jainism, Sikhism, Confucianism, Taoism, Shinto, and many others. We have seen kingdoms uprising and dissolving with time. We have been discovering new places and inventing new tools and machinery while mastering the art of medicine and science.

Though we have strengthened our core beliefs and advanced in modern science, we are yet to define life. It still stays unanswered. For now, life is a momentary experience where we come into contact with our environment, perceive it and interact with it. We are continuously changing as we go through life – growing taller, learning new things, making mistakes, and discovering more about ourselves. Some people believe that there is a Supreme Being who created everything and oversees the evolution of all living creatures. But others firmly believe that life evolves without any outside intervention.

From this perspective, science can only aid our understanding of how the world works and can never reveal everything. At the same time, science provides us with a factual foundation upon which we can build our beliefs and ideologies. It is an ongoing process as new discoveries challenge our current understanding of the universe. Ultimately, it is up to each individual to decide how best to integrate these two components in their life – science and religion – for them both to be worthwhile and meaningful.

For the believers of science and religion, it offers two vastly different perspectives on life. From the primitive man who bestowed the unknown divine forces to today's scientific methods and understanding of the world around us, judgments and beliefs have played a determining role in our development as a species. While there are times when we attempt to pit these two disciplines against each other, ultimately they work together to understand human existence.

Discussions that connect the natural sciences, humanities, and philosophy are all part of the relationship between religion and science. When we combine science and religion, we arrive at a perspective of life that helps us realize who we are and what life is.

"*In the vast playground of the universe,*
We live on an island of stars,
We call it the milky way,
There is a teeny-tiny piece of rock,

Revolving around a smaller yet bright star,
It has battled for millions of years,
And experimented with chemistry for a long time.

We... have risen from a lucky mix of organic fluids,
Multiplying every minute,
Discovering more and more,
Of what the universe has to offer.

Intellectuals, we call ourselves,
Exploring every stretch of space,

We fantasied,
We theorized,
We experimented,
And we made mistakes.

We also learned a lot,
While stumbling into surprises,
Making way for new thoughts and beginnings.

The moment of awe,
The feeling of superiority,
The growing pride,
And the infinite wealth of knowledge outside.

With all this action,
We remain calm,
Yet being hungry to know more,
About the secrets of our cosmos.

Every scientist, lawyer,
Teacher, politician, you, me and,
People from all walks of life,

Are all looking to find their purpose,
The great minds from the past,
Have been saying,
It's out there - Just keep looking."

Our ability to comprehend and control complex ideas is good enough to define the mind. But it is no longer sufficient to represent intelligence that combines the brain with judgment and care in selecting proper explanatory factors and designing empirical tests of every emerging concept.

The process of combining mind, knowledge, experience, and discretion in a way that produces a coherent expertise is the rarest of all good qualities.Wisdom requires mental fortitude and knowing the world's realities, including the limitations of one's interests and motives.

Imagine a world gleaming with humans diving right in to go deeper from our current understanding of life at an early age. We could learn about the origins of life, explore the universe and find new ways to power our devices. Science and religion have already given us so much to understand our world. Let's use it to elevate and make a real impact on society early on by understanding the basics I will walk you through in this book.

You will be equipped to blitz through the foundations early on with the confidence and mindset that you need to ponder further on these big questions of life.

There are many things we don't know, but that doesn't mean we should give up. We must continue to seek knowledge and understand the universe around us to make meaningful progress. It is not only vital for our well-being, but it is essential for society as a whole. Pursuing knowledge will help us find solutions to problems, create new technologies and improve the quality of life for all people.

Young minds like you are our future, and you have heard this "saying" a lot in many forums, discussions, media, and from parents. They are correct. You are the future, and as you grow up, we are preparing ourselves to hand over the baton of progress to you to lead on and guide the next generations for a better living. Better living is not just creating endless materialistic comforts. It is about balancing the pursuit of happiness with compassion and empathy. We all have a role to play in this. And it starts at home and goes beyond our immediate circle.

Our quest for knowledge makes us unique and what defines us as human beings. It is the engine that drives our continued progress and evolution. So be proud of your intelligence, and don't forget to use it for good!

The journey of humans as a race is mind-blowing. Even though our ancestors focussed on food and shelter, they have significantly impacted our planet. It is our belief that human beings are primates with opposable thumbs that can think ahead and plan for the future. This combination of qualities has allowed us to create civilizations, build technological wonders, cross oceans and space distances—and even alter the course of natural disasters! But it is not just our ability to make things; it is also our capacity for cooperation that has allowed us to thrive as a species.

Every day, we encounter choices. We either focus on our individual needs and try to satisfy them without regard for others, or we can work together to create a better environment for all. It is up to us as a society to decide which path we will take.

People must have access to education and knowledge to make informed decisions about their lives and the world around them. It is also essential to ensure everyone has an equal opportunity for success. We all have a purpose for being here.

You, as a human, have the power to make a difference. You can help improve the quality of life by using your intelligence and creativity to create new technologies. You can also promote humanitarian causes and work to solve world problems. The possibilities are endless! So go forth, embrace your intelligence.

- Science has given us the ability to understand and control our environment.
- Religion has taught us how to empathize with others and coexist.
- Through science, we have been able to find cures for diseases and improve life expectancy.
- We have also been able to develop new technologies that change our lives everyday.

Even after all these advances, we still live under the shadow of origin mysteries. What took place before the universe began to expand? If the general theory of the big bang is accurate, was there no matter in the cosmos until it was mysteriously created? If so, how did that happen? In many cultures, the accepted explanation is that god or gods created the universe out of nothing. However, we must now ask the next question, "Where did god come from?"

If we want to continue with this quest, why not save a step and conclude that the genesis of the universe is an unanswerable question if we decide that this is an unanswerable question? If god has always existed, why not skip ahead and assume that the universe has also always existed? Carl Sagan, a noted Astrophysicist once pointed this out.

Having spent time in the domain of art, religion, and the corporate world. I have come to an understanding that the next generation needs to focus on the questions that define each individual. Questions such as,

- What is my purpose for being alive?
- How do I connect with others to have a meaningful dialogue while I define my purpose? and
- What does it mean to be human in this ever-changing world?

The answers are within you. My effort is to enable you to extract these answers from within you.

It is up to you to continue learning about the world around you and make better choices for yourself, as your future depends on it! 'your BLACK DIARY' will introduce you to the aspects of life you will encounter as you grow. The concepts and procedures documented in this book will prepare you to wade through life's ups and downs with confidence.

The worksheets, models, and simple processes described in this book will help you in the journey of finding yourself. You will understand the true meaning of life and gain a deeper appreciation for all that you have been doing to narrow down on your purpose on this mote of dust called Earth.

CHAPTER ONE

MOVERS AND SHAKERS

Functional Brain + Knowledge (⬆) + Skills ➔ Better thinking + Value (⬆) + Common sense (⬆)

Intellectuals

Intellectuals are necessary for every culture. They contribute to the formation of public opinion or, at the very least, the public discourse on the issues that need consideration and speech. Now, who are these thinkers? What does this have to do with life? A person who values intellectual pursuits, particularly on an abstract and general level, is said to respect philosophical quests or the more complicated forms and domains of knowledge, such as aesthetics or philosophy.

An intellectual is a person who relies more on intellect than feelings or emotions; someone who is incredibly rational. Intellectuals frequently have a general or abstract perspective on life, which can help them reason through complex issues. Making informed decisions in one's personal life and public debate can benefit from knowing this.

They think differently. And can create conflict in certain situations, as others may not understand or agree with their viewpoints. However, this openness to new and different ideas is essential to any culture. The more we learn and grow intellectually, the better equipped we are to address the challenges of today and tomorrow. The impact of intellectuals on our lives is evident in their ability to think critically and engage with complex issues. They provide a perspective that can help us make informed decisions, whether it is about what we eat, how we live our lives, or the policies and civil rights that govern us. Further, they apply their expertise in the political sphere, which turns into workable policy alternatives.

Noam Chomsky famously quotes - *"Optimism is a strategy for making a better future. Because unless you believe that the future can be better, you are unlikely to step up and take responsibility for making it so."*

All our purpose in life leads us to become intellectuals in our fields. When anything is perceived intellectually, we see from the conscious mind and ordinary awareness, which entails analyzing, contrasting, drawing conclusions, reasoning, planning, and decision making. Intellectuals have well-organized and disciplined mindsets. However, it appears complicated to an outsider. If you are looking at honing these skills, you need to be patient and have realistic expectations to realize your vision.

Yes! Things will be difficult initially, but try not to get upset. Imagine how marvelous things could be if you only took the necessary action to make them happen.

Also, dogging your goals, especially when it initially seems unachievable, persistence is essential.

However, to become an intellectual, you must adopt a combination mindset. What does that mean? It means we must nurture Trust, Value, Courage, Positivity, Learning, Patience, and Focus. I know it seems excessive, but everyone is capable of living this combo. This mindset is only possible when you have integrity, empathy, and humility. You can do this, trust me.

In the end, I have dedicated a chapter describing each mindset with a process.

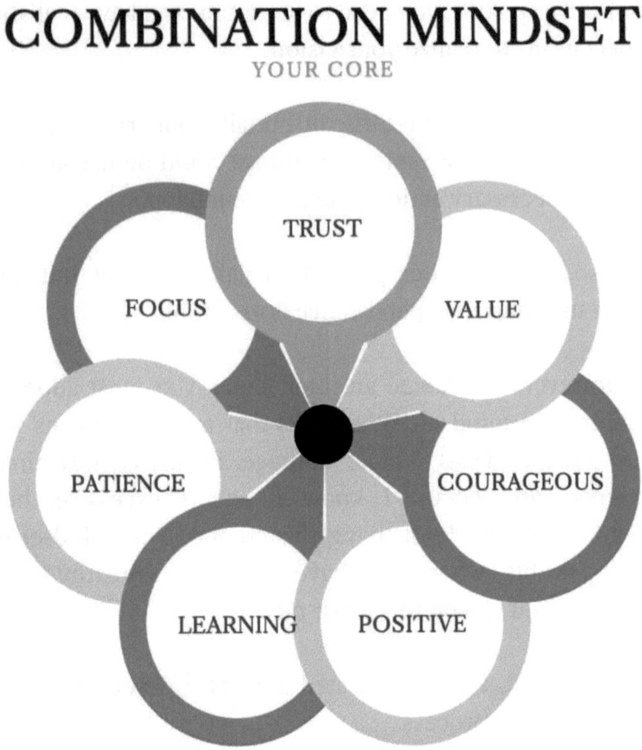

COMBINATION MINDSET

YOUR CORE

TRUST
FOCUS
VALUE
PATIENCE
COURAGEOUS
LEARNING
POSITIVE

Figure 1.0 - Core Combination Mindset

If you are willing to advance intellectually, you must cultivate cognitive or open-mindedness skills to improve your capacity for thought and reasoning. If you are reading this book, that means you can think. Now, it's about how you structure your ideas, opinions, and perceptions to make sense of the environment in which you live. You must evaluate information critically and draw valid conclusions independently, creatively, and imaginatively. That is why we have our brains, let us put them to proper use.

Most importantly, you must have a passion for learning – whether about current events or something more esoteric or theoretical. It's not enough to know what you're talking about; you need to be able to communicate your knowledge articulately and interestingly as well. Finally, persistence is essential: if you don't succeed at first, keep trying until you do. There are many influential intellectuals in our lives. They spent their lifetime polishing these skills. Some of the most well-known names include Albert Einstein, Leonardo da Vinci, and Isaac Newton. Now, take out your phones and search for public intellectuals like Sunita Narain, Peter Singer, and Martin Rees. Each of these individuals had a profound impact on the world around them – and not just intellectually but also socially and politically. You will join the club if you spend the time nurturing the combination mindset.

One reason their contributions are so significant is that they break through traditional boundaries of thinking. They challenged accepted wisdom in their respective fields, which led to discoveries and a greater understanding of humanity. It is ultimately what makes intellectuals so important – they are individuals who help us to see the world in a different light, and that's why their contributions are so invaluable. Imagine, ten years from now - you have nurtured the combination mindset tirelessly and entered the feeling of ultimate accomplishment of being an intellectual.

Earlier, we spoke about cognitive or open-mindedness skills. You can develop it through education (not limited to academics) and exposure to different disciplines. Studying philosophy, sociology, mathematics, or physics may lead to an appreciation of the complex nature of reality, which in turn will help you think more critically and logically.

Additionally, reading diverse texts – both popular and academic – will broaden your horizons and allow you to see the world from a variety of perspectives. There are plenty of excellent books available on Amazon that you can read and gain different perspectives on various topics. The idea is not to restrict yourself to academic boundaries. Expanding your knowledge will help you stand out from the crowd and foster a more open-minded attitude. When you combine all these skills, you become an intellectual – someone who can think critically, understand complex issues, and see the world in a new light.

Let me remind you, being an intellectual isn't just about having a high IQ; it's also about your curious mind and a passion for learning. It's essential to be willing to explore new ideas and concepts, no matter how challenging they may seem. If you can build a strong foundation in your intellectual pursuits, then you're well on your way to becoming an influential individual in your own right.

Here are 5 simple steps to increase your intellectualism. Tick (✓?) how many you are already doing.

- **Read a variety of books:** Less fiction and more thought-provoking concepts. Pick up any excellent book, say climate change, for example.
- **Debate to discuss:** When you have discovered a concept that sparks your interest, meet the like-minded and exchange thoughts to deepen your understanding.
- **Train your mind:** Consistently enable your mind to think differently and out of the box.
- **Multilingual:** Engage and learn new languages and scripts to expand your reach to deepen your thoughts on the chosen concepts.
- **Hobbies:** Develop a practice of hobbies and physical exercise. It will refresh your mind to think better.

Intellectuals' impact on the society

In the early days of civilization, intellectuals were often the ones who discovered and popularized new knowledge. The role of intellectuals has always had a profound impact on society, often leading to social change. They helped to shape the way people thought about the world and the way they lived their lives. Today, intellectuals play a significant role in society by providing insights into myriad topics. They often challenge accepted assumptions and ideas, helping to spark change and make society more informed.

Thomas Sowell once said, *"There are only two ways of telling the complete truth-anonymously and posthumously."*

While there is no one definition of an "intellectual," anyone who pursues deep and challenging intellectual pursuits can be said to be influencing society in some way. Broadly they are divided into two main categories: scholars and thinkers. Scholars often focus on acquiring new knowledge, while thinkers use this knowledge to explore ways of its application. In either case, their impact on society is intense because they help to shape our understanding of the world around us.

Are you an intellectual? If so, do you have these traits?

- Do you have a deep and curious mind?
- Do you question all aspects of life?
- Are you highly analytical when evaluating your thoughts?
- Do you find it easy to break down complex problems into simpler pieces?
- Are you creative and come up with new solutions to longstanding challenges?

If you have answered yes to the above questions, you are on the right track - stay focused. If you answered no to any, there is nothing to worry about. You can start by nurturing the combination mindset to head towards becoming an intellectual.

But how? Let's deep dive into the basics, preparing you to develop this wizardry mindset.

CHAPTER TWO

DISTRACTED MINDS

Technology + Smart Usage ➔ Focus (⬆) + Me Time (⬆) + Distraction (⬇)

The powerful mind is something that everyone desires. It's the ability to control your thoughts and emotions, think deeply and creatively, and achieve goals. But what happens when your attention shifts constantly from one task or activity to another? Your mind becomes scattered, and you will feel lost in your work or life.

2020-2030 is a Techade, meaning a decade with a high impact of technology while being human-centric. Undoubtedly technology has been dictating the social construct and has rooted its presence in every profession and household. It is now the basis of human conversation and interaction. You and I are dead-set obsessed and pride ourselves on flipping and scrolling through endless applications. Why not - technology gives us the power to accomplish a heap of tasks with little time.

With the advancement of technology, we witness the rise of distracted minds in the younger generation. All thanks to the multiple channels of stimulation bombarding our senses at once. Our attention span has been declining with our increased undesired fixation on technology.

In this age of technology, our gullible minds become easily distracted. So, it's vital to be selective about the information and stimuli we allow into our minds.

Distracted mind

They are interruptions. Anything that takes your attention away from your work or the task at hand is an interruption or distraction. It can be something as simple as a phone ringing, a notification popping up, a friend visiting, or a busy environment. The problem with distractions is that they can keep you from completing your school work or task justly, leading to mistakes and lost time.

Do you also feel that you are not in a position to focus on anything these days? Whether it's school, family, friends, or your hobbies, it seems like there's always something pulling you away from what you're supposed to be doing.

Here's a theory about why you get distracted - it's all about your concentration. Aah! You knew it was coming! When you try to focus on one task, there is always something vying for your attention.

Here's a list of some of the most common reasons for distraction that you experience:

1. **The need for instant gratification** - When you're faced with something you want or need, your instinct is usually to grab it and move on. It can be especially true when it comes to food.
2. **The need for novelty** - When something is new, it's more exciting and captivating. That is why new movies, games, and products are often so popular - they offer a sense of novelty that can be hard to resist.
3. **The need for stimulation** - When we're bored or stressed, our brains naturally turn to things that will provide a temporary burst of excitement or relief. It can include watching TV shows or surfing the internet, among others.

Activity 1:

Use the table below to list down your specific distractions and score them against their importance and the effort required to get rid of them.

DISTRACTION PRIORITY INDEX

DPI

TOP 5 DISTRACTIONS

#	DISTRACTION	IMPORTANCE	EFFORT TO REDUCE
1	Notifications	__/10	High / Med / Low
2	Social Media	__/10	
3	Texting	__/10	
4	Gossip	__/10	
5	Friends	__/10	

LIST YOUR DISTRACTIONS

#	OTHER DISTRACTIONS	IMPORTANCE	EFFORT TO REDUCE
1		__/10	
2		__/10	
3		__/10	
4		__/10	
5		__/10	
6		__/10	
7		__/10	
8		__/10	
9		__/10	
10		__/10	

Activity 1: Score your distraction

Some common distractions that can hamper productivity and creativity include:

- Checking social media
- Texting or emailing
- Watching TV or browsing the internet
- Working on a project that's not related to your work
- Working on a project that's not specific to your skill set
- Working on a project that's too large or too difficult
- Making decisions that are not based on evidence

Distractions can come in many forms - from work, social media, and other things we take for granted.

Distraction Priority Matrix (DPM) helps you visualise the importance of your distractions based on the score you arrived at using the Distraction Priority Index (DPI).

DISTRACTION PRIORITY MATRIX

DPM

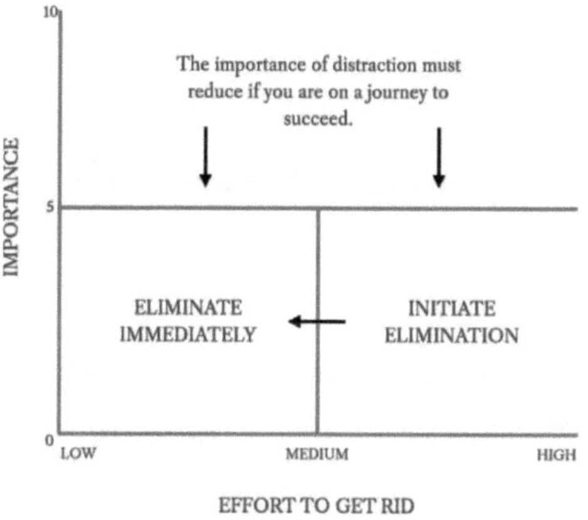

Figure 2.0 - Distraction Priority Matrix

Activity 2:

Using the above DPI score, plot them on the Distraction Priority Matrix.

YOUR DPM - WORKSHEET

PLOT IT NOW

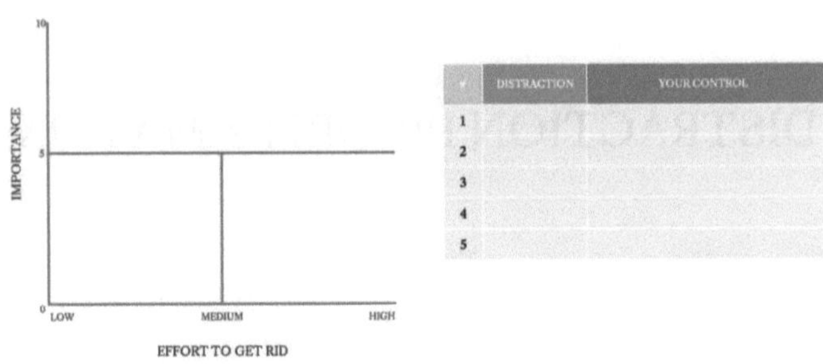

#	DISTRACTION	YOUR CONTROL
1		
2		
3		
4		
5		

Activity 2: Plot your scores

Check out an example of the matrix which I used years ago and helped me.

KRISHNA'S DPM

2012

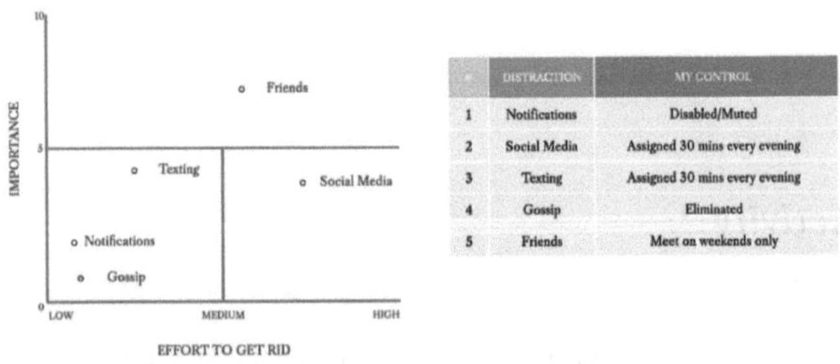

#	DISTRACTION	MY CONTROL
1	Notifications	Disabled/Muted
2	Social Media	Assigned 30 mins every evening
3	Texting	Assigned 30 mins every evening
4	Gossip	Eliminated
5	Friends	Meet on weekends only

Figure 2.1 - Example of Distraction Priority Matrix

Activity 3: List outcomes of your activity.

#	DISTRACTION	YOUR OUTCOME
1		
2		
3		
4		
5		

Activity 3: List the overall outcomes of your activity

The impact

Distracting thoughts has a HUGE impact on your productivity and overall your life. It can often cause you to make careless mistakes, be less careful in your activities, and waste time trying to fix things from the past. Internal distractions often cause you to focus less on the task, leading to sub-par work and rushed projects. External distractions can have even more lasting effects - they steer you away from your goals and fill your time with things that are not beneficial to you or important in your life.

A wandering mind teaming with mental distractions disables your power to perform deep work. Your cognition shifts ceaselessly from one task to another, pushing you to become sluggish. You suffer from shoddy thinking, poor problem-solving skills, and a lack of focus and creativity. Your rumination power fails, leading to negative thoughts and a vicious cycle of disorganization.

Distraction saps your cognitive resources by robbing you of attention spans that can last for hours or days at a time. Take a look at some events in your past. Are there instances where you still have some pending tasks that you must have closed already? Have you ever wondered why? Yes, this is the long-term distraction you are facing due to lethargy or procrastination that has kept you away from completing these tasks.

The problem with distraction is that it can harm your growth and overall well-being. Be aware of these specific impacts of distraction:

1. It can lead to decreased focus and concentration.
2. It can lead to decreased productivity and increased boredom.
3. It can lead to decreased efficiency.
4. It can lead to decreased creativity.
5. It can lead to decreased decision-making skills.
6. It can lead to decreased problem-solving skills.
7. It can lead to decreased ability to learn new information quickly or effectively.
8. It can lead to increased anxiety and stress levels.

The list can go on. There are many reasons why distraction is a huge problem. It slows down your cognitive processes. It can also lead to problems with memory and multitasking, which can be incredibly dangerous when it comes to work and school. In the worst case, it can also lead to addiction and mental health issues.

So, what can you do to protect your ancient brains from distractions?

The first step is to be aware of the problem. That means being honest about how much distraction you experience and how often. The distraction priority matrix you just plotted will help you narrow it down.

It also means setting reasonable limits on how long you allow yourself to be distracted and sticking to them. Finally, it's essential to train your brain in ways that will help them resist distractions - this includes learning how to focus and stay organized, as well as developing good habits for thinking straight and staying calm under pressure. With these tools in hand, you can help protect your mind from unnecessary distractions - and emerge stronger mentally in the end!

Thus, it's crucial to be mindful of your surroundings and use distractions only when necessary. If you find yourself struggling to get focused, try taking some time for yourself - go for a walk, read some literature, or take a break. Just make sure that you come back refreshed and ready to work!

The power of the mind

You agree that the mind is capable of incredible things while it evolves. Studies have shown that the power of the mind impacts your physical and emotional well-being. It can help you achieve goals and improve your productivity, as well as your relationships with others.

Though it may seem rough, controlling your thoughts is a skill you can gradually develop over time. These pointers will help you better understand what the mind is capable of:

1. **You can train your mind to do just about anything** - With enough dedication and effort, you can coach the mind to achieve the impossible.
2. **Your mind is constantly learning** - The more you discover, the better the mind will become at learning new things. Keep your brain active by reading books, understanding new concepts, and participating in various activities that challenge your mind.
3. **Your mind can heal itself** - Yes, your mind is capable of healing itself if you allow it to do so. Remember: there's no limit to what the mind can achieve!
4. **Your mind is capable of making connections** - With the knowledge you gather, your mind can grasp new information quickly by making connections between previously learned information and newly found information.
5. **Your mind can form ideas** - Ideas are bits and pieces of information. Blend them well in a way that makes sense to you.

6. **Your mind can solve problems** - Problem-solving skills are innate. When you experience tasks or situations that require you to think outside the box and figure out a solution, your mind finds solutions. So enable your mind and expose yourself to these situations more often to encourage problem-solving skills.

7. **Your mind is capable of manifesting** - With effort, anything that you desire if you set your intention and believe in it strongly enough. It manifests.

So, while your mind is powerful and worth exploring more closely, it's vital to use it in the best way possible for your mental and physical health. Just remember that everything starts with a thought - so start with a positive one! And then - practice, practice, practice - that's the key!

Ruling Your Distraction

Once you understand how distraction works, you can use this knowledge to your advantage. The key is learning to identify which thoughts are harmful and disruptive and then block them from entering your consciousness. It is easier said than done, I agree. But there is a way to win over your distractions and rule them.

You see, controlling your distractions is easy when your mind is focused. It means you must identify which thoughts are harmful or disruptive and either ignore them or banish them systematically.

Also, your brain is constantly processing information. Even when you're not actively thinking about something, your brain is still working on it. Become aware of when your mind is wandering. When you become aware, it's harder for your thoughts to take control and force themselves on you.

It is the inevitable nature of the mind to get distracted, but you have the choice to choose against it and command your mind to stay focused. With practice, you will master your distracted mind and gain control over it.

There are many different ways that you can do this. One approach is to use the distraction transition model. It is a simple 3 step process that you can implement with ease. Again, you must commit to practicing this technique if you want to be successful.

Distraction Transition Pattern

Use the Distraction Priority Matrix outcomes that you have plotted. Identify distractions that you wish to kill.

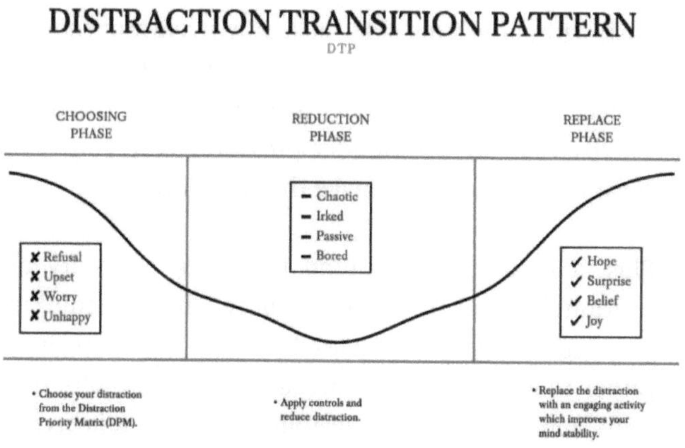

DISTRACTION TRANSITION PATTERN

DTP

CHOOSING PHASE

REDUCTION PHASE

REPLACE PHASE

✘ Refusal
✘ Upset
✘ Worry
✘ Unhappy

– Chaotic
– Irked
– Passive
– Bored

✔ Hope
✔ Surprise
✔ Belief
✔ Joy

• Choose your distraction from the Distraction Priority Matrix (DPM).

• Apply controls and reduce distraction.

• Replace the distraction with an engaging activity which improves your mind stability.

Figure 2.2 - Distraction Transition Pattern

While you use the above transition pattern, it is essential that you also keep the below points in mind.

- Be organized.
- Take breaks.
- Practice self-discipline.
- Use technology in moderation.

The benefits of a non-distracted mind are manifold, and they go beyond just being able to focus better. You can own your mind by learning how to control your thoughts and emotions.

There are several reasons why a non-distracted mind is so powerful. For one, it allows you to stay focused on the task without getting sidetracked by irrelevant thoughts or distractions. It gets easier to complete difficult tasks or projects while being productive throughout the day. It also helps you stay calm under pressure. Worrying about irrelevant things will only make the situation worse.

Plus, a non-distracted mind promotes creativity and innovation because it leads to more creative thinking. When your thoughts are focused on what you're trying to do rather than thinking on unrelated matters, you're more likely to come up with new ideas and solutions. It is because your brain is clear from thinking about mundane things that don't have anything to do with the task.

Look! Owning your mind by learning how to control your thoughts and emotions is one of the most powerful tools that you can have in your arsenal. It will allow you to achieve seemingly impossible goals while remaining calm and collected under pressure – essential qualities in any successful individual.

Some takeaways:

- *Increased productivity.*
- *Improved focus and concentration.*
- *Effective learning of new concepts.*

For parents

If you are a parent reading this book and wondering how you get your child involved to reduce the distraction. Start with making your child aware of new-age distractions like smartphones and over-exposure to technology. It will vary depending on their age and developmental stage.

Consider this. As a parent, I am sure you know that there's nothing more frustrating than witnessing your child crying uncontrollably. It feels like their pain is completely overwhelming, and you just want to do something to make it stop.

It is a common experience for parents, and you also experience this often and turn to your smartphones for help. Silently distracting crying kids with their flashy screens, you can momentarily take away the pain and allow them to calm down. It's so easy for you to succumb to the temptation of ignoring the children's cries - because you believe it's easier to give them the smartphone than to engage with them emotionally. Think! Are you one of them?

Parents must learn how to handle difficult situations with their children effectively - without relying on technology. By expressing empathy and understanding through words instead of flashy screens, they can help build a strong relationship with their children that will last long into adulthood. Spend time with your kids and consider these tips that will help:

1. **Discuss new age distractions with your children** - Talk to them about all the different things they can be doing online other than engaging deeply in social media and why you think they might be fun or educational. Let them know that you are there to help them stay safe, but also make them aware that you're also willing to let them make their own decisions. But do not be overprotective. You will deny a learning opportunity for your child by doing so.

2. **Avoid judgment** - It can be tough to keep our opinions to ourselves, but it's important to do so when it comes to children. You need to provide them with a safe and nurturing environment where they can explore their interests freely. Next time when you tend to judge or make a comment, think again about the impact.

3. **Empathize** - One of the most important things you can do as a parent is to empathize with your children. It means understanding where they are coming from and what they might be feeling at the moment. When you know them better, it makes it much easier to set boundaries and live in harmony together.

4. **Teach values and meditation** - Above all else, you must introduce your child to values and morality. These are the foundations of a successful society, and we need to instill them early on for them to form healthy habits for life. Also, engaging children in meditation and mindfulness practice at an early age is beneficial for their body, mind, and soul.

5. **Encourage creativity and imagination** - By letting them create their own stories or art, they will start to

embrace their inner creativity. Over time this becomes a default mode network and strengthens their ability to think better and solve problems.

At the end of the day, modern technology is a boon, maybe. It also disables the mind of its thinking capacity by engaging your child in activities that harm their overall development. You must enable the children to think more deeply and better understand the world around them.

CHAPTER THREE

Concentration and Self-Discipline

Focus (🡅) + High self-discipline ➔ Definite success

How often have you heard your parents or teacher say - "Concentrate while you are studying"? Plenty, right? I heard it almost every other day from my parents. At first, I thought that I was doing something wrong! Later I understood that I did not know the meaning of concentration. Relatable?

Argh! The word concentrate was the key word during my childhood, and it upset me almost every day. Why?

The reason why concentration is so important during your childhood years is that you are still learning how to focus. When you are young, it can be hard for you to stay focused on anything. Your prefrontal cortex (the part of the brain responsible for planning, controlling, and inhibiting impulses) hasn't fully developed yet. It means that when you try to focus, it can be difficult because your instinct is to wander off.

Simply put, concentration is the ability to focus your attention on a specific task or goal. When you can focus, it allows you to accomplish tasks with ease. The secret to success is concentration and self-discipline. We need to learn how to focus so that we can achieve our goals. Concentration is simple when you follow the process. The process (Fig 3.0) has worked for me for many years.

Always break down your goal or target state into daily activities. The reason we do this is to manage our day and time. You, me, and everyone else have only 24 hrs every day. So, make sure you plan the activities to fit into your schedule with buffer time for any uncertainties. Don't stuff your calendar to choke yourself.

At first, you may find it difficult to focus. It may feel overwhelming, and your mind pushes you to give up. That is a natural reaction. Think of it this way, when you can do an additional rep in the gym even when your arms are in pain, why not push yourself to focus a little more, fortifying your mind? It is a similar mindset or the mantra successful people use. To make it easier for you, follow the below quirks, which will help you build this routine.

1. **Practice focusing for short periods** - When you first start practicing concentration, try focusing on a single task for just 10 minutes. Gradually increase the length of time

until you can focus on a task for an hour or more. It will increase your willpower.

2. **Practice focusing in different environments** - Sometimes, practicing concentration in different setups is helpful, such as at home, at work, in a noisy environment, and so on. It will help you become better at switching between different situations and staying focused while managing distractions.

3. **Use relaxation methods** - Some people find it helpful to use relaxation methods before trying to focus on a task. It can range from deep breathing exercises to visualization techniques. Experiment and see what works best for you.

4. **Practice multiple tasks at once** - Try and practice concentrating on multiple tasks simultaneously. It will help you learn how to juggle many thoughts and stay focused on the activity.

5. **Using dual n-back tasks** - Dual n-back tasks are a type of cognitive task that demands both memory recall and attention. When you train your brain with this type of task, you will improve your concentration and increase your attention span.

With the constant bombardment of marketing campaigns for new products or services, stylish men and women flaunting their figures on social media, cute pet videos, and other breaking news is undoubtedly a temptation to break your concentration. Maintaining self-control with dedication and putting in the hard work without excuses is necessary for consistency.

Ultimately, it is up to you to decide if you want to fall prey to the distraction or realize that the distraction is worth nothing to your success and keeping the focus. That is where self-discipline plays a role.

Concentration Model

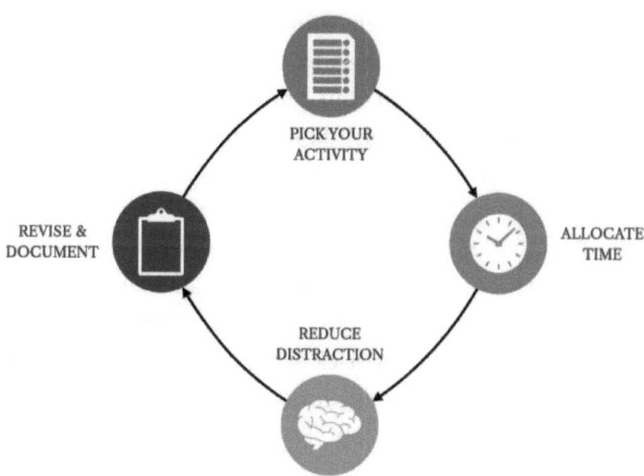

Figure 3.0 - Concentration Model with focus cycle

Sometimes there are days when you cannot concentrate whatsoever due to some unforeseen events in life. It is natural. Not every day will be 100% productive, and not always you can stay highly focused. Then you must follow the below mind detox procedure to recharge yourself.

1. **Get enough sleep (I know it's your favorite)** - Studies have shown that getting enough sleep is essential for overall well-being. It can also help you stay focused and concentrated. Try to get at least seven hours of sleep every night, and avoid caffeine and other stimulants before bedtime. And for those who love sleeping, don't overdo it.

2. **Exercise regularly** - Many people think exercise is good for staying fit physically, but that's not the only benefit - it has also been shown to improve focus and concentration. Make sure to include some form of cardiovascular activity in your routine at least three times a week. You will find a shelf full of books teaching you how to do it. Shamelessly explore them.

3. **Practice meditation or mindfulness** - These are ancient practices, and even today, we all love practicing them. It improves our focus, concentration, and moods overall. Sitting with your back straight and breathing deep 20 times for 5-10 minutes works like magic and you will feel rejuvenated immediately. Try it.

4. **Make a list of what needs to be finished** - When I'm working on any project, I always list activities that I need to do and how I need to do them. It helps me stay organized and avoid any time-consuming backtracking. Also, it helps me ease out any panic I might have. ;-)

PS: *It takes time and practice to reach optimum focus levels for every individual. So the key is to maintain high self-discipline* *and follow your routine.*

Activity 1: List down all the activities you are currently involved in and mark their importance with a reason. Use arrows to indicate the priority.

FOCUS PRIORITY LIST - WORKSHEET

YOUR PRIORITIES

Activity	Importance	Why? (Your rationale)

HIGH ↑ NEUTRAL ↔ LOW ↓

Activity: List down all the activities you are currently involved in and mark their importance with a reason. Use arrows to indicate the priority.

Activity 1: List your priorities

Self-Discipline

You may want to be the richest or one among them with all the comforts around you. You may want to reach the top of your professional ladder, or you may want to get the highest grades at school. Any long-term goal that you have thought of or dreamt of requires self-discipline. Discipline is the ability to control your actions and behavior in the face of temptation. It is the crucial ingredient for achieving the desired success through practice. That means every individual on this planet can become successful - it all boils down to how disciplined you are. When you discipline yourself - you can stay on track and achieve your goals.

But, these days, you and all the others are attracted to bypass methods. Additionally, there are so many side hustle opportunities that float around on social media and the internet. Some claim to just log in to a particular website and become rich. Some say upload videos to streaming platforms and become famous. The people who are marketing these tactics are also victims like you.

Look around, and you will find 9 of 10 not disciplined with the growing independence and self-reliance. That is a clear opportunity to become disciplined in your chosen area and shine brightly.

Successful people in any field have put in a lot of effort and are self-disciplined in their approach and methodology. That is why they are famous and have attracted a following. You might now point out the viral ones - what about them? I would compare these to lottery tickets. How often do you win them? There is no guarantee that you will become successful through any of the shortcuts. It is possible to lose a lot of money and time with them.

If your long-term goal includes becoming rich, there are certain things that you need to do to achieve it. It includes developing an entrepreneurial mindset and setting goals accordingly. Market yourself effectively by creating valuable content. Network and build relationships with key individuals who can help promote your business. And be resourceful in finding new ways to monetize your business.

Remember, there needs to be **value** in whatever you put your heart into.

Being disciplined is important for any skill you plan to master or learn. For example, if you want to be a great musician, you must practice your instrument every day. If you dream of being a great basketball player, you must practice your shot every day. And, if you want to be a great writer, write every day. Discipline is the key to perfecting any skill or talent you may have. There are no shortcuts in life to achieving success - and that is the slap-on-the-face fact.

The same principle applies to any activity you perform at school or work or even when you volunteer for a local community. I have seen and met a lot of rich people. They have money, wealth, and all the comforts the world can offer. But, they are unhappy. Many of these rich people think that they are not yet successful. If you are one of them, you'd agree with me on this without a blink. Being rich and famous is not the end goal. A knowledgeable and humble person is. If you have the knowledge and self-discipline - wealth and fame are just bi-products. Aim to reach here.

SELF-DISCIPLINE
INFINITY MODEL

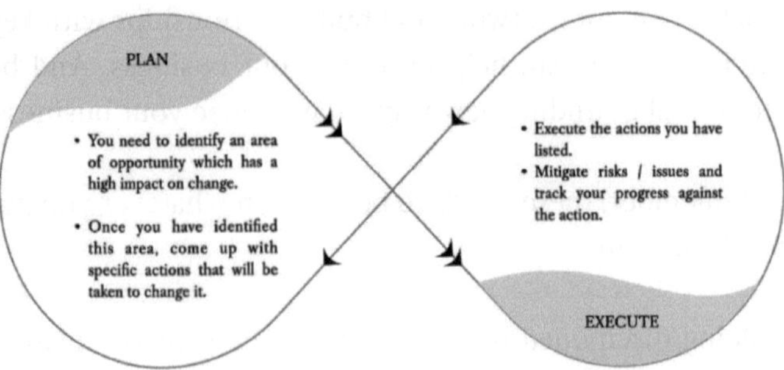

Figure 3.1 - Self-Discipline Model

Self-discipline dimensions

There are many dimensions of self-discipline that you will have to master if you want to achieve long-term success. These disciplines are the ones that make you an unbeatable force in life:

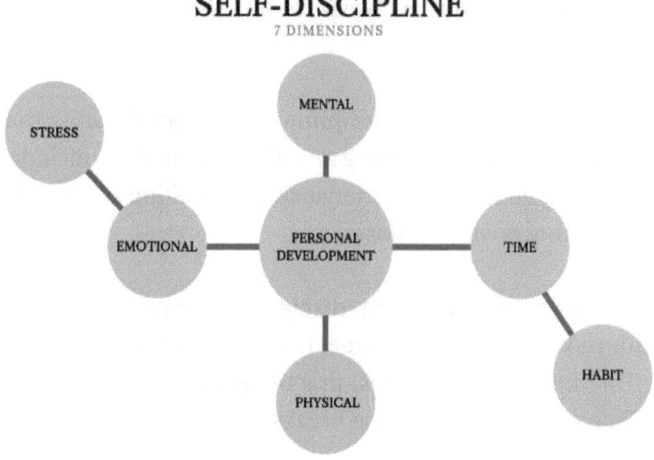

Figure 3.2 - Self-Discipline Dimensions

1. **Mental discipline** - Stay focused and motivated when things get tough. It involves developing a powerful work ethic and sticking to goals, no matter how difficult they may seem.

2. **Physical discipline** - Create habits and develop exercise schedules that help you stick to your daily routine and achieve your fitness goals. Do it repeatedly.

3. **Emotional discipline** - Regulate your emotions and stay calm in difficult situations. It's important to have a healthy sense of self-awareness and to handle stress healthily.

4. **Time management discipline** - Manage your time more effectively to achieve your goals. Set realistic deadlines, plan your day/week/month wisely, and create a to-do list.

5. **Habit formation discipline** - Form good habits that will help you achieve your goals. Habit formation includes developing good organizational skills, breaking bad habits, and creating positive habits.

6. **Stress management discipline** - Manage stress to achieve your desired outcome. It includes strategies such as setting healthy boundaries, practicing meditation/prayer/stretch exercises and taking breaks regularly.

7. **Personal development discipline** - Expand your knowledge and skills to achieve your goal. It includes strategies such as reading self-help books, attending workshops/classes, and getting training from a qualified individual or organization.

Visualize the impact when you are self-disciplined

Imagine what might happen if you shape your attitude, emotions, and behavior and become disciplined. You will be the master of your mind and will have the complete authority to design your progress. Self-discipline will affect your personality astronomically. And the most empowering thing of all - you'll see results that reflect positively on who you are. You will,

- Become a master of self-control and willpower.
- Build your self-esteem and confidence.
- Boost your creativity and motivation.
- Improve communication and teamwork skills.
- Improve problem-solving skills!

Now, become successful.

Yes, self-discipline is a winning skill. It's one of the most important skills you'll need if you want to be successful in anything. Once you've determined what you want to achieve, set smaller, more manageable goals that you can accomplish. This way, you won't feel swamped and discouraged when you look at your larger end goal and realize that it's still too big to tackle. After you've set your smaller goals, break them down into more manageable tasks that you can complete regularly. This way, progress is consistent, and you'll stay motivated.

Putting a schedule in place for your goal will help you to accomplish and realize the outcomes. This way, there are no surprises and no excuses that you can give yourself!

Among us are a few who need a push at times. So, have a friend, family member, or colleague aligned to your goal to give you that necessary boost. It is difficult when you first start working on improving your self-discipline. Don't get discouraged - just remember that it takes time and patience to change habits. There will be setbacks, but keep pushing forward using the focus techniques.

If there is no discipline, what will happen is that your mind will eventually become ungovernable. It will lead to chaos, as different ideas and thoughts try to assert dominance over the others. There could also be uproar as individuals try to take what they perceive to be their rightful place in the group. In the end, your mind would most likely dissolve or fragment. I don't think you would want to end up like a chaotic mind soup (laughs).

Rewiring your mind to reach your goal

For any successful student, it's essential to develop healthy habits that will last a lifetime. If you are a student, it is the right time for you to start developing a strong sense of self-discipline. It helps you to achieve your goals and stay on track. It's also essential for you to become successful in any field - from business to academia. Here are some key reasons why self-discipline is so important:

1. Self-discipline allows you to set and achieve goals.
2. Self-discipline helps you to stay focused and motivated.
3. Self-discipline allows you to resist distractions and temptations.
4. Self-discipline leads you to better study habits and improved performance in school and other areas of life.
5. Self-discipline provides a sense of accomplishment and control over your life.

6. Self-discipline creates balance in your life and helps you focus on priorities.
7. Self-discipline leads you to a healthy mental attitude, which is essential for success.

Self-discipline is not only for students and children. It is for anyone who wants to enjoy a sorted life - it allows you to reach your goals, stay focused, resist distractions, study well, and have a positive attitude towards your prospects. So be sure to develop good habits early in your educational/work journey, and you will be well on your way to success!

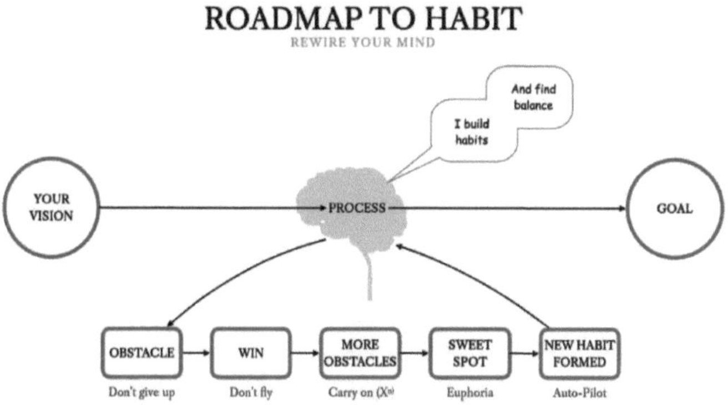

Figure 3.3 - Roadmap to Building Habit

If you understand the 'why' behind your behavior, you will find it easy to gain control over yourself. That is when having a good understanding of motivation comes in handy

- knowing what drives you. To ensure that you are creating good habits, try to create rituals around your goals (viz., setting a daily or weekly routine) and establish positive reinforcement mechanisms (viz., rewarding yourself after reaching goals). Too much self-discipline can lead to burnout, while too little can lead to relapse. Finding the right balance is important, so you don't overdo it or give up on your goals altogether.

CHAPTER FOUR

PRINCIPLES AND ETHICS

Principles + Morals ➔ Strong Character

At a young age, you are impressionable and open to new ideas. You are also eager to learn and develop your morals and values. One way to help you imbibe principles and ethics is to model them yourself. As young children, doing the right thing is important, no matter the consequences. Your parents often share their values and standards with you, so you know what to expect from them.

You must also understand why it's essential to stand up for what's right – even if others don't agree or think it's necessary. Developing strong ethical beliefs is an ongoing process, but modeling good behavior and instilling a sense of fairness will go a long way for you when you grow up to be a responsible and ethical individual in civil society. Therefore, you must be exposed to good moral development early on.

Candidly, let me put the three principles and ethics in front of you that you can imbibe in your young mind:

1. **Honesty** – Honesty is one of the most important principles that should be deep-rooted in you. It's not only necessary for personal well-being but also essential for building trust and credibility. Furthermore, it is crucial to develop a firm moral code.

Be truthful and fair in all your dealings with others and yourself. If you're always lying or hiding things from yourself, it'll become tough to be sincere and fair when dealing with others. When people are honest, they build relationships of trust and respect with others, which leads to a more harmonious and productive society.

Being honest doesn't mean you have to tell everyone everything that's going on in your life - you should keep some things hidden for your safety and privacy. But at the same time, you should never withhold information from those entitled to know it (like friends or family).

If you are a parent or teacher, there are many ways to teach honesty to children, but the most effective way is probably by example. Show your kids that honesty and uprightness is the best thing by living it yourself! If you say something you don't believe or know is true, then be upfront about it and let them know why you feel that way. It will help them learn to be truthful in all situations and build strong moral values.

Honesty is like a muscle. The more you use it, the stronger it gets.

2. **Compassion** – If you are from this planet, then you can show compassion. As simple as that. It is the feeling of sympathy for other people when you understand their feelings and perspectives. Showing compassion towards others makes them feel appreciated.

When you have compassion for others, it is easier to empathize with them, build trust, and help them solve their problems. It is essential in difficult situations – like when someone is in pain or facing a difficult challenge.

For example, when we're compassionate towards someone, we tend to treat them with respect. It makes our conversations more productive and positive, as well as helps us build relationships that are durable over time. Furthermore, behaving kindly towards others can encourage them to do the same.

It's also important to develop compassion for yourself. You realize that you're not alone, no matter how tough things may seem. And this helps keep you motivated and focused throughout your journey. Beyond just being polite and ethical, compassion also has tangible benefits.

Like Arthur Schopenhauer quotes, "Compassion is the basis of morality." It leads to increased happiness and satisfaction in life. It can also encourage kind actions towards others, such as donating money or time to charity. In short, compassion increases your well-being and the well-being of those around you.

Compassion is like a baton in a relay race. People will always pass it on.

3. **Integrity** – Living up to your word is essential for maintaining trust and credibility. People will respect you more if they know you are reliable and honest- even in difficult situations. Integrity is the principle that all individuals need to adhere to maintain ethical behavior. It refers to the fair treatment of others, regardless of their position or status in society.

It involves maintaining your values and standards no matter what, which means you won't compromise them for anyone or anything. You also have to be able to admit when you're wrong, apologize sincerely, and make amends where necessary.

Integrity is also about doing what's right even when no one is watching or judging you. For example, if you tell a lie intending to hurt someone else, you'll still have violated trust even if they never find out about it. It is important to have strong values and ethics and to share them with others. It will help them understand and live by them. Always aim to become a steward of integrity.

Integrity is like trust; you can lose it in a wink of an eye.

Morally inclined routine

I will keep it plain and simple. As humans, your moral obligation is to imbibe the principles and ethics that guide you in life. These values help you make sense of the world around you and help you live ethically. They also provide guidelines to behave as a good citizen and uphold justice. You learn these principles better when you expose yourself to different ideas and perspectives early on in life. Go out and explore the range of opportunities available for you on various concepts. It will help you develop a broad understanding of the world, and eventually, you'll start making better decisions.

Once you know the principles and ethics, it's important to be critically minded. You have to be willing to question everything you believe in. Otherwise, your ethical ideals will become shallow and easily compromised. As with anything else in life, there is no one correct answer - only different perspectives that can help you learn more about your world and yourself. And because knowledge is power, nothing beats having access to as much information as possible! Think critically not just about what people say or do - but also about the evidence that supports their claims.

The world is constantly changing, and so are your values and ethics. If something doesn't work for you anymore, you must be willing to let it go. You can't cling to things that no longer serve you or help you grow - you need to move on to become a better person as you inch towards adulthood. It isn't always easy, but it's an important part of developing integrity as a person. If you ever face a difficult decision, remember to consider what is right and wrong, as well as your values. If you have practiced self-discipline, you will one day think of becoming an architect to change the way we live and make it a better place for the next generation.

Being ethical means standing up for what you believe - even if it's unpopular. Sometimes speaking out against injustice can be scary, but it's important to do whatever you can to help. It doesn't matter who you are or where you come from - everyone can make a difference. And that starts with speaking up when you see something wrong happening.

People often think of ethics as rigid rules and regulations, but that's not always the case. Sometimes the most ethical thing to do is go against what you believe and protect another person or situation. As long as you're honest with yourself and your decisions, experimentation is key - it can help you learn more about who you are and what you value.

Also, being truthful is the best way to protect yourself and others. If you're dishonest or selective with your information, it can lead to problems. You need to be honest with people - not just about what you know but also about who you are and how you feel. Honesty isn't always easy, but it's an important part of building trust - and is essential for lasting relationships.

One of the best things you can do for yourself gives time. That means nurturing your well-being, both mentally and physically. Being grateful not only makes you feel good inside, but it also helps you be more considerate and generous towards others. It's easy to get caught up in your everyday lives, but taking time each day to reflect on what you have - and don't have - can help you be happier and more fulfilled.

Principle, Moral, Ethics - what and why?

Principles, morals, and ethics are all related concepts that can be difficult to distinguish from one another. They all play a role in guiding our actions, but they differ in how they do so. Principles are general rules or guidelines that we use to make decisions. They are the absolutes, such as "honesty is the best policy."

Morals are more specific guidelines about what we should and should not do, based on our values and beliefs. For example, most people would likely agree that lying is wrong.

Ethics is a broad term that refers to the principles and morals we use to live our daily life. Say, for example, fairness, compassion, and responsibility.

Your parents and teachers have learned all of this on many different occasions. You must continue learning and growing as a person. It's not only about acquiring new knowledge but also about applying and sharing it in the most effective way possible. One of the ways to learn and grow is through experience. As you get older, your experiences can help you develop empathy and understanding for other people.

You can also learn how to problem solve and make wise decisions in difficult situations. Experiences also help to reflect on what matters most and what you're willing to stand up for. Overtime you will realize that,

- You have built a strong character.
- You can distinguish right from wrong.
- You boost your self-confidence and positivity without a fight.
- You have started to shape your attitude, belief, and behavior.
- You ward off negative peer influence on your own.
- You lend your support in difficult situations.
- You build better relationships with others.

The good mix

Apart from the **THREE** must-follow hardcore principles (Honesty, Compassion, and Integrity), give equal care to the below morals for you to become a respectable human.

Gratitude: Be sure to take time each day to reflect on what has gone well, and let those positive emotions guide your actions and thoughts moving forward. Maintain authenticity.

Equality: Treat others with the same level of respect and kindness that you would want to experience yourself.

Acceptance: Even though we sometimes resist change, be open-minded and learn from others. What you think is right may not be the same as what others believe.

Generosity: Your selflessness and giving back to society must be the mantra. Be it through helping others or simply by being friendly.

Responsibility: When something terrible happens, don't blame others – the first step is to take ownership of your decisions and learn from them.

Perseverance: Go the extra mile when faced with any obstacle. Make it your way of life.

Self-control: It's one thing to be able to resist temptation, but it's another thing altogether to control your emotions and impulses. If you can avoid succumbing to the strong desires of your heart, you'll be a step closer to becoming a successful person.

These character traits shape you into a better person and make you less likely to succumb to negative peer pressure. Imbibe these soon, as they'll form an indelible impression on your mind and will be easier to stick with in times of stress or temptation.

Collective ignorance of principle and ethics

There is a growing trend in the social construct of people wanting to remove morality and principles from their lives. Often in the name of "freedom." That isn't freedom - it's chaos. Individuals without principles and morals are more likely to be selfish and destructive. In our increasingly fast-paced and complex world, it's more important than ever to instill positive values in young minds. Principles and ethics are two vital aspects of a sound moral compass. And if they're not nurtured and respected, chaos will ensue.

Without principles, you would be unable to make moral decisions or stand up for what's right. And without ethics, there would be no way to determine whether your actions were ethical or not. It is important to remember that principles don't come pre-packaged with a set of instructions on how to follow them. They must be learned through experience and education and applied consistently to achieve results. This process can be complex at times, but it's well worth the effort if you want to grow into an exemplary citizen who knows how to act ethically in any situation.

Don't wait for external motivation - It's purely DIY (do it yourself)

Oftentimes we find ourselves lost, stuck, and tired of worldly issues. If you haven't faced them yet, you will surely do. There is no escape, it is a natural process in the journey towards success, and that's okay. The sooner you learn to embrace this, the better off you'll be. Successful people are not those who wait for others to hand them success - they achieve it through hard work and dedication.

It is critical not to give up or become complacent in your pursuit of success. If something is worth doing, it's worth doing well - no matter how difficult it may seem. That doesn't mean becoming a workaholic; instead, it means setting a high bar for yourself and meeting it no matter what. When you're putting in the effort, it's easy to taste success.

It's okay to make mistakes - Everybody does! Remember that failure plays a significant role, and it is not bad; it's an opportunity for growth. It can teach you a lot about yourself and how you can improve your skill set. I would argue that failure is one of the most important aspects of personal development. You will learn more about how failing can be fun later in this book.

But, for now, how do we motivate ourselves in the face of an obstacle?

Motivation is an important aspect of any effort - whether you're trying to lose weight, finish an assignment, or start a business. There are many different ways to motivate yourself. Don't fret too much. Motivating yourself is the best way to get back on track and is effortless when you give yourself time. Remember, your mind is in your control. You are not a puppet of your mind. So, take ownership and dictate affirmative terms to your mind. See the change when you do it. You will be surprised!

Start with,

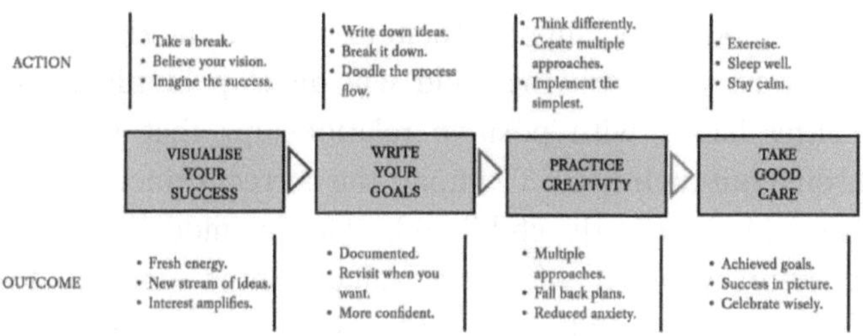

Figure 4.0 - Self Motivation - DIY Workflow

1. **Visualize your success** - When you feel low about your progress or motivation, try visualizing yourself achieving your goals. It can help to trigger positive emotions and help you stay focused on your outcomes.

2. **Write down your goals** - Keeping a journal is a great way to keep track of your progress and stay motivated. Writing down what you've accomplished can also help to boost your self-confidence and remind you why you're doing all this hard work in the first place.

3. **Get creative** - Sometimes, a simple change of scenery helps you get back on track. If working inside feels like a drag, try going for a walk, taking a bath, or reading something creative for inspiration.

4. **Take care of yourself** - No one succeeds alone, and taking care of your mental and physical health will help you reach your goals faster and with less stress. Make sure to get enough sleep, eat healthy foods, and exercise regularly.

For parents

If you are a parent or teacher, guide the younger generation as role models and support them to walk on the right path. This way, your growing child will develop humility and healthy habits with positive relationships that will last throughout their lives. To impart the correct principles and ethics in their early childhood, start by modeling these behaviors yourself with core values. Show empathy for others, act with integrity, and always put the needs of others before your own. It is a teachable moment that you must not let go of. Furthermore, enforce rules through logical reasoning and consistent discipline. If you can instill these values early on in a young person's life, they will be more likely to adhere to them throughout their lives and find contentment.

Children must learn the importance of integrity to be moral and ethical citizens. These **FIVE** simple methods must help you.

1. **Model integrity yourself** - Instil a strong sense of honesty, decency, and respect for others by setting an example for yourself. It will encourage the children to do the same and build a sense of social responsibility.

2. **Set rules and guidelines** - Clearly define acceptable and unacceptable behavior and enforce them consistently. It will help children learn early about the consequences of breaking the rules.

3. **Encourage creativity and imagination** - Let your children explore their creativity by encouraging them to use their imagination for constructive purposes, such as making up stories or creating art. It will help foster a sense of individuality and uniqueness.

4. **Teach life lessons** - Discuss essential life lessons with your children, such as how to deal with difficult situations or be compassionate towards others. It will help them develop good judgment and maturity.

5. **Reinforce the importance of honesty** - Constantly remind your children that honesty is the key to a healthy relationship, career, and social life. It will help them develop strong moral values and stay true to themselves.

Activity 1:

Using tally marks, ask your friends/parents/teacher to score you on the morals. Show off once you have completed the activity.

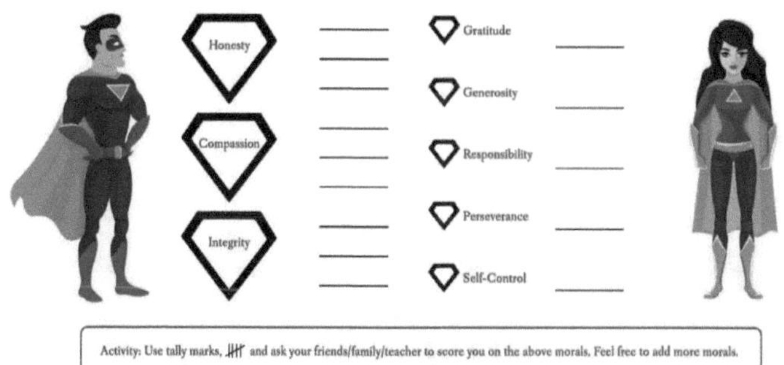

Activity 1: Document what others think about you

Activity 2:

Build your tree of morals. Fill in the bubbles with the morals you acquire from activity 1 of this chapter.

Activity 2: Build your tree of morals

CHAPTER FIVE

PURPOSE

Purpose + Dedication ➔ Mastery + Peace

It is all about the meaning, connection, autonomy, and significance. Don't we strive for this every day in one form or the other? I do. I look for the meaning of my existence. The connections I make are for a reason. The independence that I gift my mind is precious, and of course, I look for a significant impact on my presence even after I'm gone. Don't you also think of it?

In many ways, but at its simplest, the purpose is why we are here. It's what drives us and helps us to live our lives in the right way. Find a way to express your purpose if you want to stay motivated and inspired throughout your life. It could be something as simple as volunteering for activities or working towards a larger goal that you believe. Whatever it is, make sure you keep it close to your heart so that you can always find strength in it.

The purpose itself is a big topic, and one can interpret it in myriad ways. But you understanding your purpose is the critical part of finding your path. Simply put, it is all about your personal goal or mission that you feel passionate about. It can be anything from satisfying your needs and desires.

Finding purpose in life is one of the most important things that you can do, and it's something that everyone should consider at some point in their lives. Purpose can take many forms, but it's usually best to think about what you want to accomplish with your life and then figure out how to get there.

There are many resources available online that can help you find your purpose. You can read articles, enjoy listening to podcasts, or watch videos on the topic. You could also do some soul-searching and write down your thoughts and feelings about what matters to you the most. You know that is the best option - your purpose should come from within. That is when it has a meaning that connects with you deeply and motivates you when you need it. It is like your best friend living inside you.

Whatever route you choose, ensure that you are constantly growing and evolving as an individual and continue strengthening your purpose in life. If you're not sure what your purpose in life is, then you're not alone. Many people feel lost and don't know where to start. Finding your purpose is a daunting task. But it's worth taking on if you want to live a happy and fulfilled life.

Some questions for you to reflect on,

- What does life mean to you?
- Why are you here?
- What makes you happy?
- What do you want for yourself?

When you ask these questions daily, one part of your mind will stop you. These are difficult questions, and your mind will try to pull you away from them. It will prompt you to give up by using distraction tactics. But it is your willpower and self-discipline that should keep you powering. Nothing has stood victorious against willpower and self-discipline. As you master them daily, your mind will start to answer these questions. That is when you begin to see a hazy picture of your purpose. That's hope. That's you finding the glimpse. When this practice becomes a habit, you will have discovered your purpose.

Busy is the world so much,
We hardly get to think worthy as such,
Minor and piffling thoughts occupy the mind,
"Our Purpose" always gets thin lined!
We all talk about freedom from the rest.
Give it a thought, have we freed our minds at best?
Looking back from the time we became wise,
Does it look too far from the skies?
It's time to choose what we think,
Guide our minds to be in sync,
"Peace" is what we all need.
Focus the mind and gracefully kneed!

The purpose is like nurturing a tree to grow. Once you have identified or have a notion of your purpose - consider it a sapling, and it needs to grow. The key is to keep watering the sapling daily with your focus and dedication. As you continue living with your purpose, it will blossom into what we call Ikigai (Japanese for "reason for being"). In Japan and worldwide, Ikigai is a much-loved concept. Ikigai is a deeper understanding and realization of one's reason for being. It happens gradually over time, while other times - that might be sudden and seemingly out of nowhere. The important thing is that you have pursued finding your Ikigai continuously throughout your life.

Remember, the journey is more important than the destination. The most important thing is to keep moving forward even when things get tough, even when you don't know where to turn. Don't be afraid to change your direction and try new things, as long as they align with your purpose. As you keep growing and learning, you will stumble upon the right path - leading you to where you must be. Find your Ikigai, and live with purpose every day.

2 part plan for you to maintain your purpose journey.

Part 1: Finding

1. **Reflect on your past** - What were some moments in your life when you felt the most connected? What were some things that you enjoyed doing? Answering these can help you identify your values and motivations and start to build a plan based on those things.

2. **Ask yourself questions** - Once you have understood your values and motivations, ask yourself questions daily. These questions should help you stay focused and motivated throughout the day. Some examples of good questions to ask yourself include: "What are my goals for today?", "What would make me happy?" and "What is my contribution?".

3. **Get creative** - If you struggle to find inspiration, get creative! Try painting, writing, or designing something new. When you're able to let go of the limitations that society has on you, the sky is the limit. Remember, many times, your hobby might become your passion and may give

you a sense of direction leading to your true purpose.

4. **Join a community of like-minded people** - Finding your purpose is tough, so connect with the workforce who share similar values and common goals for help. Group activities such as volunteering or being part of a social group will help you meet new people and build relationships that support your goals.

5. **Set milestones** - One of the best ways to stay focused on your goal is to set milestones along the way. It will give you something tangible to aim for and progress each day. Some good markers to include are: making a significant contribution to your community, learning new skills, or reaching a personal weight goal or fitness level.

Part 2: Growing

1. **Be willing to change** - Just because you've found your purpose doesn't mean that things will be easy! You will have to make some changes along the way to achieve success. That includes cultivating healthy habits and setting boundaries with negative people and situations. Don't be afraid of failure - it's all part of the journey!

2. **Reflect on your progress** - Once you've reached some milestones and achieved a certain level of success, take the time to reflect on your journey and show gratitude. It will help you stay motivated and focused as you continue down the path toward your purpose. Ask yourself: "What did I learn today that I can apply to my goal tomorrow?" or "How can I improve upon what I've done so far?"

3. **Be prepared to change again** - Just like life, your pursuit of purpose is full of twists and turns. As you continue on your journey, you're likely to encounter new challenges that will require some additional adjustments to

succeed. Don't get discouraged- these changes are part of the process!

4. Seek out advice - Along the way, it's a good idea to seek advice from those who know more than you about your goal – your family, friends, professionals, or online resources. It plays an important role. Getting outside feedback will help you make better decisions and stay on track toward success.

5. Cherish the journey - Remember that what matters most is not the destination – it's the journey itself! Making progress each day is an accomplishment and deserves to be celebrated!

As you grow older, you'll realize that the world is your playground. You have the power to create whatever life you want, and there's no limit to what you can achieve. So don't be afraid to take risks and venture into new territory. Be open-minded and trust your intuition because it will guide you toward the correct path.

Another important thing to remember is that your work is never complete. The reason why we're here on Earth isn't just for selfish reasons – it's so that we can help others and make a difference in the world. So don't settle for anything less than fulfilling work that guides you to a positive impact on humanity or nature. And finally, don't forget to enjoy the journey! Life is too short not to live it fully!

Your purpose is unique to you.

Yes, each of us has a unique purpose in this world. We were all created with a specific set of skills and abilities that we can use to help others and make the world a better place. We can use our unique talents to create businesses that help others, work in charities that assist those in need, or plainly make a positive impact on the lives of others.

Your purpose is constantly evolving. As you grow and learn more about the world - your purpose will continue to evolve. You'll start to see yourself as a connector - Someone who can help connect people to create positive change. Whatever your path, ensure to stay true to who you are and what makes you unique so that you can create the possible impact in this life.

There is no 'right' way to do any of these things, as what makes one person's 'purpose' different from another is purely up to them. The important thing is to identify what makes you happy and then put your heart into doing the things that help you realize your success.

That is the key to living a fulfilling life - find your greater sense of purpose, and embrace it wholeheartedly!

Creating your Chakra of Purpose

Core outcomes

The core outcomes are the parameters that interlink the aspect of Meaning, Connection, Autonomy, and Significance to arrive at your purpose. Creating your Chakra of purpose will help you to identify and connect with the things that are important to you, create meaningful connections with your purpose, have a great deal of autonomy in your life, and make that significant impact that you dream of. Follow the below method to create your Chakra of purpose.

Meaning:

To strengthen your purpose, the first thing you need to identify is the meaning of your life. Why are you here? What is it that you want to achieve with your time? How can you contribute to society?

Discover your meaning in life through introspection and self-reflection until you find a sense of meaning. There is no right or wrong answer here. Everyone has a unique path to follow to find meaning in life. The important thing is to keep an open mind and allow yourself to grow along the way.

Activity 1:

List down your thoughts on what could be your meaning of life in the below table and rank their priority to you.

WHAT GIVES YOU MEANING?

WHAT GIVES YOU MEANING?

#	DESCRIBE THE MEANING OF YOUR LIFE	RANK	WHY? - WHAT IS YOUR RATIONALE?
1			
2			
3			
4			
5			

Activity 1: What gives you meaning?

Fill in a rationale as to why you have chosen these

priorities. It will help you connect back to your thoughts and change them later (if need be) when you have polished your meaning.

Connection:

One way to connect with life is by finding your passion. What does this mean for you? It means you should identify something that interests you and learn more about it. That means reading books, watching documentaries, or spending time discussing the topic with other people. The key is to find something that motivates you and start young, whether it's personal growth or helping others.

It becomes much easier to find things you're passionate about and to connect those passions with the things you do.

Activity 2:

List down your thoughts on what passion connects to your meaning in life. Use the below table and rank their priority to you.

WHAT IS YOUR PASSION?

WHAT IS YOUR PASSION?

#	DESCRIBE THE PASSION THAT CONNECTS TO YOUR MEANING.	RANK	WHY? - WHAT IS YOUR RATIONALE?
1			
2			
3			
4			
5			

Activity 2: What is your passion?

Autonomy:

Let's be frank, most of us fail to think about our purpose beyond the basic needs we need to survive (like food, clothing, and shelter). Is that the end of the road? Ask yourself!

Unlearning what we know and welcoming new knowledge enables your mind to upgrade constantly. When you are in the habit of enhancing your thoughts, you create space for new and better ideas to enter your life.

You learn more about yourself when you challenge what you know. When this happens, it exposes the limitations of your current perspective and forces you to rethink everything from scratch. It is a powerful technique that can help you grow in many ways - not just mentally but emotionally too.

With regular practice, your mind will become capable of thinking out of the box. You experience a new wave of thoughts that surprises you.

Activity 3:

MAKING SPACE FOR NEW LEARNINGS.

MAKING SPACE FOR NEW LEARNINGS.

#	LIST WHAT YOU CAN UNLEARN / SHARE WITH OTHERS?	WHAT NEW CONCEPTS YOU WISH TO LEARN?
1		
2		
3		
4		
5		

Activity 3: Make a wish-list of new learning

Significance of Impact:

Now that you have listed your thoughts and interests in your passion. Find out what is happening around you related to your pointers and research it thoroughly. This way, you will recognize the great potential and how your actions can help effect change.

The world is constantly evolving. So, be open-minded about what's happening to stay ahead of the curve. When you see something that needs improvement, take action and make a difference!

When making a real impact on society, sometimes all it takes is one person who listens and learns from others. Before long, they may inspire others to also take part in making an impactful difference.

Now, complete your mandala with the outcomes of your activities. Fill each layer with your meaning, connection, and autonomy. This is your personal Chakra of purpose. Keep revising!

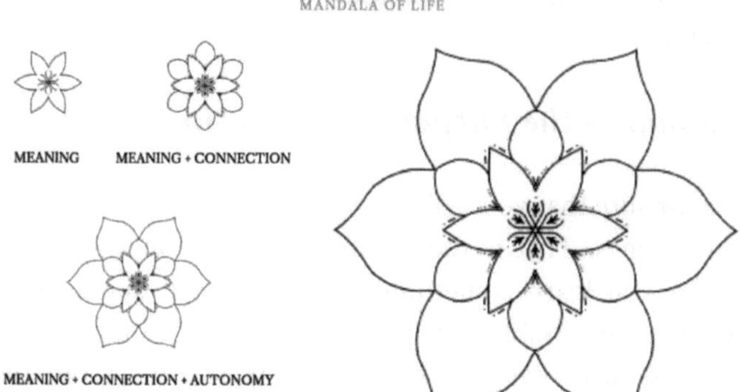

Figure 5.0 - Purpose Chakra

In reality, once you have identified your life's purpose, you will live it. Of course, there are obstacles and victories along the journey. You must keep adjusting and moving towards your goal until and unless an event in your life forces you to change your course completely. But, even then, your general purpose in life will not change. It is just the pause you are experiencing, and soon you will be back on track to living your purpose.

Sometimes, you may feel like you're on track and that living your purpose is a natural progression. On the other hand, you may feel completely lost and don't know where to start. The key is to keep listening to your intuition and gut instincts and never lose faith in yourself. If it feels right, then it's probably right. You'll find your way - Just stay open to possibilities!

Revisit your Chakra of purpose and perform the exercise again. You will see that you will now have an updated version of the Chakra, which is more stable and meaningful.

Managing the purpose upgradation.

It is for sure that you will edit your purpose Chakra at least a few times. That is the nature of purpose and learning. When you learn something new - purpose upgrades to become more stable. If you find that your life purpose has changed, it's vital to take some time to reflect on this change and figure out how you want to implement this change. Here are a few things to keep in mind if your life purpose changes:

1. **Talk to friends and family** - Your loved ones will be the best resource for helping you figure out what you should do next. They may have experience or knowledge you aren't aware of, and they will undoubtedly be supportive of whatever decision you make.

2. **Seek professional advice** - If you're feeling stuck or unsure about what to do, consider seeking professional advice from a career counselor or other specialist in your field. They will be able to help you explore all of your options and come up with a plan that is tailored specifically to your needs.

3. **Get started on research** - Once you have a good idea of what direction you want to take, start doing a preliminary study into the various options available. It will

help you figure out which path is the best for you and save you from making an uninformed decision later on down the road.

4. **Be patient** - Upgrading your life purpose may take some time, but eventually, you'll reach your destination. Remember that everything will happen in its own time, and there is no need to rush things - Just take it easy and trust the process.

Imagine life when you have mastered your purpose.

It is the dream of every person in this world to fulfill their purpose. When you have fulfilled your purpose, you'll feel like everything in life is worth living. You'll be happy and content. You'll know that your work is meaningful. You'll feel a sense of satisfaction and fruition that can last a lifetime. You won't need to worry about anything else in the world because you'll have found peace and fulfillment.

When you wake up each day knowing exactly why you're doing what you're doing and are excited to get started - this is when you've mastered your purpose. When you no longer have to think about your purpose or what you're supposed to be doing - this is when you've reached a level of mastery. And, if you find yourself questioning your purpose or how to improve - that is an indication. You still have some work to do. Keep pushing yourself and try to reach new levels of mastery!

CHAPTER SIX

EMPLOY SILENCE IN LIFE

Silence + Time ➔ Self-Discovery

Employing silence in your life is a powerful way to explore your deeper self. It can help you connect with your emotions and instincts and tap into your creative capabilities. When you remain silent for extended periods, you free yourself up to focus on the thoughts and feelings that lurk under the surface.

Silence allows you to uncover hidden insights and memories that you might not have been able to access before. You will also connect better with other people more authentically because of less inhibition by social norms and conventions.

By letting go of the need for constant communication and engaging with others, you will focus on important aspects that concern you. It will allow you to come into contact with parts of yourself that you may have neglected or been afraid of in the past. As a result, you will discover new perspectives and ideas you would never have thought possible.

Silence also allows you to build stronger relationships with those around you. The base of these relationships will be trust and respect, rather than forced interaction or superficial interactions. That is why it is essential to find a way to incorporate silence into your life gradually – so that you don't feel the burden or a limitation. Once you are familiar with its benefits, it becomes an essential part of your routine!

Employing silence can help you achieve greater levels of clarity, insight, and motivation.

But why the silence?

Imagine you have the freedom to choose chaos and peace. You would select 'peace' - a human instinct. Isn't it? Silence helps you evoke a particular emotion in anyone around you. There are many reasons why silence is crucial, and it has a role in all aspects of our lives.

Tick (✓?) which of these have you already experienced?

- Has silence helped you to focus and concentrate?
- Has silence enabled you to be creative and productive?

- Has silence helped you reflect on your thoughts and feelings?
- Has silence helped you meditate or pray?

Both literally and figuratively, silence is necessary. It will help us focus, get creative, and reflect on our thoughts and feelings without intrusion! It also improves our mental health.

In the spiritual world, one practices silence through meditation and contemplation. It is often associated with stillness, peace, and tranquility. When you are in silence, you are in that particular moment, and you will focus on your thoughts and feelings without distractions. It is a way to connect with yourself and gain insight into your spirituality.

In your world (if you are not a silence practitioner), you can adopt these simple techniques to practice silence.

Shut up: Yes! You have to shut your mouth, literally. Some of us feel the need to keep speaking to stay energetic. They believe that endlessly talking is the only way to stay afloat in the chaotic world and for people to listen to you. It is not. Are you one of them?

Calm your mind: Take twenty deep breaths, and focus on your breathing. Notice how your stomach rises and falls with each inhale and exhale. I am not going to teach you meditation. But, when you observe your breathing, you gift yourself the time to focus on your breath which calms your mind. That is my intention here. When you are calm, the worldly noise will become less overwhelming.

Eliminate distractions: Turn off all electronic devices, put away all printed materials, close the door of your room if possible (this helps block out auditory pollution), etc., to get into "silent mode" more easily. Silence is a great way to focus and improve concentration.

Get out of your head: At first, you will fall prey to your thoughts. They tie you up and behave in a possessive manner. You will get lost in thought. Whenever this happens, mentally recite the alphabet or any other helpful phrases. It will help you break the chain of thinking about specific things and also help keep your mind clear!

Meditate: If you are unfamiliar with meditation, just sit for a few minutes in silence and focus on your breath. Try to be present at that particular moment and allow yourself to drift away from any thoughts or concerns that may come up. Focus on your surroundings, and interact with them.

Create your rituals: Create a custom that you enjoy and find calming, such as spending time in nature, reading a favorite book, or listening to music. Taking yoga classes is also a great way to explore more of the therapeutic benefits of silence.

When you're silent, you're allowing your inner voice to speak. This voice is the part of you that's compassionate, creative, and wise. You will find it chaotic and jumbled with numerous thoughts, but stay with it. It happens when you are beginning the process. It gradually allows you to be in tune with this voice. And help you to make more informed decisions and to develop your intuition.

PS:*If you can be in tune with the worldly matters outside, tuning with your mind is a walk in the park.*

A gateway to mindfulness

You might have heard about mindfulness in various texts. It is a practice that helps us to be more present at the moment and to focus our thoughts and feelings without getting caught up in them. Silence plays a vital role in practicing mindfulness and opens a gateway to your deeper self. According to experts, the time spent in silence can help you connect with your inner voice. That's why embracing silence is such a step in cultivating mindfulness skills! Consider it.

There are many benefits that you can harvest. Most importantly, you can reduce stress, anxiety, and depression, while improving your focus, concentration, and problem-solving skills. Such a sweet replacement, isn't it?

There are many ways to practice mindfulness. And one popular way is to listen to soulful music. Music provides a gentle background sound to help you focus on your breathing and calm your mind. You must have tried it already!

Remember - mindfulness is not a magic bullet - it is just a medium to help you focus on your thoughts and feelings healthily. If you find that it reduces stress or anxiety levels, then continue it.

When embracing silence, start by simply committing to spending five minutes each day in complete stillness. If this is too difficult or uncomfortable, try listening to calming music instead. Ultimately, the goal is for you to progress gradually and allow yourself time and space to experiment with mindfulness skills. I will be surprised if you are unable to dedicate these five minutes.

Strengthening communication using silence

Here is the magic of silence! You can convey the strongest of messages by being silent. When I was young - I often flinched and failed to realize the power of silence. Mostly because communicating with others scared me. However, now, silence is a powerful tool for me to explore my deeper self and communicate stronger messages.

There are several reasons why I failed. First, I felt overwhelmed and sucked up in a vacuum with random noise or chatter when communicating with someone. As the years progressed, it allowed me to decrypt, and I started paying more attention to the other person and hearing what they were saying. It was only because of focus methods that I had applied to break down the noise, chatter, and complex messaging into meaningful matters.

That is why it's often easier to understand complex ideas when you're able to focus on the individual words rather than on the overall message. You must have experienced it too.

Furthermore, silence gives you time to think about your response before saying anything. It allows for a more thoughtful reply that will be less likely to be interrupted or changed by irrelevant thoughts. Finally, silence provides space for both parties involved in a conversation to listen without feeling pressured or judged. It's a way of communicating that allows everyone involved in the exchange to feel heard and respected.

So if you're looking for ways to explore effective ways of your communication, silence is the way to do it. Try it. It's a medium that allows you to communicate thoughtfully and meaningful way. It will lead to stronger connections with others.

The importance of silence in you.

When you employ silence in your daily life, your actions become more controlled and grow the potential to connect with everyone and everything in the world. When you're able to find golden moments of silence, you will connect with your emotions and memories more easily. It will become your magic tool for self-reflection and growth.

In addition, when you learn to find moments of silence, you will train your mind to be more focused and alert. It will help you to live a more mindful life, leading to greater happiness and satisfaction.

Here are some reasons why must silence is so important to you:

1. I find that silence helps me clear my head and focus on the task. It's simple, but it works - I've found that when I'm in a state of silence, I'm more productive than when I'm not.

2. Silence has a soothing effect on me, which allows me to relax and recharge my batteries. That is especially important during times when I'm stressed out or overwhelmed.

3. Silence allows me to think more deeply and creatively - when I'm in a state of silence, I can access my subconscious mind more easily. It allows me to come up with new ideas and solutions to problems I may not have thought otherwise.

4. Silence forces me to be introspective, which can help me reflect on my life and learn about myself. This process is often uncomfortable but ultimately rewarding, as it helps me grow.

In short, silence is a powerful tool that can help you achieve your goals professionally and personally. If you're ever feeling lost or stagnant, try taking some time for yourself in silence to get back on track!

Exploring inner self with silence

Silence can help you clear your mind and focus on your thoughts, feelings, and sensations. You can also allow yourself to process these things without any distractions. It involves focusing your thoughts on one or more specific topics or concepts and then holding on to those thoughts for some time. It allows you to understand yourself and your emotions. In addition, it helps cultivate calmness, introspection, and patience.

By learning to silence the voices in your head and focus on one thing at a time, you'll be able to better connect with the things that matter most to you. Here are some ways that silence can help you explore your inner self:

1. Silence can help you to focus and concentrate.
2. Silence can help you to become more aware of your emotions and thoughts.
3. Silence can help you to figure out what you want or need.
4. Silence can help you to connect with your intuition or inner wisdom.
5. Silence can help you to develop a sense of self-awareness and understanding.

Positive modification of behavior

By now, you have understood that silence can foster introspection. It's no wonder that it can also help you to modify your behavior as well. With practice, you will start seeing changes in how you behave and approach your life. You will find your situational awareness and decision-making skills improving. You will understand the concepts with better quality and clarity.

It is a new world altogether that you will explore when you employ silence in your daily routine. People around you will start to respect who you are. While you understand yourself better, your focus grows deeper into thoughts and feelings without interruption. You will analyze them better by building stronger relationships with them.

Eventually, these changes will reflect in your physical behavior as well. You will control your speech and body language and experience a boost in your confidence. You will start to see positive changes around you benefiting your progress towards your purpose. You will be eligible for all these just by employing silence in your routine. Would you want to give it up? Think again!

Remember, your journey in life is all about trial and error. Once you know yourself, you'll be able to experiment with different areas without worrying about how others might respond. So, silence is not only a tool for introspection but also for positive behavioral modification.

CHAPTER SEVEN

INDEPENDENT LIVING

Independent Living + Will Power (🡅) 🡆 Simple Living + Personal Growth

Let me put it out straight - Independent living is a lot of responsibility and accountability for any actions you perform. First and foremost, if you are thinking about embarking on an independent life, there is no doubt that you will need plenty of self-reliance - both mentally and physically. You will find relying on yourself for food, shelter, clothing, etc., which can be daunting.

On top of that, independence comes with its own bunch of challenges and worries - like how will I afford my bills or where will I live? - Do these questions pop into your mind too?

I didn't mean to scare you! And, there is nothing to worry about. Look around you - many started to live independent lives when they attained adolescence. All you need is a bit of effort and perseverance. You can make the dreams of independent living a reality.

Elements of an independent life

From parents or school, you must have learned about basic living needs. Apart from food, clothing, and shelter, you must secure a firm hold on your physical, mental, social, and financial needs before you reach adolescence. It should be part of your developmental psychology. To live without dependence, you'll need to have enough money saved or invested to cover basic expenses. You'll also need some skills or knowledge you can sell or use in your profession. And finally, you'll need to be comfortable living in a harsh environment – where you may not have access to the usual amenities (like clean water or reliable electricity).

Many deceptions circulate in social media about simple living in the wild or the mountain villages. They claim to earn by doing freelancing or something similar. Indeed, people live there, but you are not aware of the struggles that you may have to go through on a typical day.

At the same time, claiming to be a "wild primitive" or living off the land (as depicted in movies) is not realistic and can lead to hardship, disease, and even death. Don't be stupid to try these without preparing yourself. It requires years of mental and physical preparation to change your lifestyle if you are accustomed to living in the cities.

In fact, only a small percentage of people who attempt independent living can survive long-term without assistance from outside sources. The rest eventually return to mainstream society in search of comfort. Some even become homeless due to a lack of skills, money, bad luck with weather patterns, etc.

So if you want an adventure – and I think people do, introduce yourself to all these aspects and prepare well. It's not easy, but it can be gratifying. Minimum dependency is living without the help of others for at least six months. If you want to live independently and have a low or no reliance on others, then you set some fundamental prerequisites first.

It includes becoming as self-sufficient as possible, learning to live without modern conveniences, and setting realistic goals. If you're thinking of trying it out, start slowly by living on less and gradually increasing the challenge over time. There is no right way to do this; everyone needs to find what works for them.

The most important things are discipline (keeping a schedule), focus (sticking with your goals), and patience (taking things one step at a time). It's also helpful if you have some wilderness experience because this can give you an edge in adapting quickly to new surroundings.

Once you have these prerequisites in place, there are a few different ways to live independently. You could live in an isolated location where it's hard to get help if needed or set up a small outpost in an urban area where you can still connect with the rest of society. Or maybe you're more comfortable living alone in the woods or on an abandoned island – whichever option is best for you!

Despite the challenges inherent in living independently, there are many benefits to this type of lifestyle. For one, it gives you freedom and flexibility. You're no longer beholden to anyone else, allowing you to live the life best for you. Furthermore, it allows you to connect with people from all over the world – which will broaden your horizons and enhance your understanding of human nature.

I will share an incident. When I was young, I hardly knew how to prioritize my activities. I spent a lot of time doing odd jobs and arranging cultural activities, apart from studying. My performance was dull, really dull. I failed to give the required focus or attention to myself or to what I was doing. All my activities were scattered.

One day my spiritual teacher saw me and made me sit with him. He looked at me for a while and said nothing. I started to grow uncomfortable, and in a low voice, I asked - Did I do anything wrong today? He smiled and said - *"Listen to me carefully. Take a break for six months and go away somewhere and do nothing. You will realize."*

I sat there confused and unaware of the context. After this episode, I continued the way I was. But, in the back of my mind, his words puzzled me.

You might think that this changed me at that moment. In fact, no! It did not. I chose to ignore him completely. It took a few years for me to realize what he had said.

So, my advice is to learn from the mistakes of others. And do not ignore the advice from your parents or teachers. Prepare yourself as early as possible.

There is a growing trend among people who want to live independently – without relying on anyone else. This lifestyle can be liberating and allows you to pursue your interests and passions without constraints. I am not suggesting you run away from home and start living. That would be the worst piece of advice.

In fact, an act of craziness without planning is stupidity, but a well-planned crazy-act is a game changer. So, be wise and plan well.

You need to do detailed planning and have the immense willpower to live your dream of being independent. You must make sure the transition is smooth from your current status to the new way of life. Onboard your family members, friends, and well-wishers in the process and have them accept your way of living and your decisions without causing any ripple in their lives.

Being independent is the ultimate freedom that you must strive for. There are several benefits to living an independent life. You can live in the moment and experience life to the fullest by giving more time to understand your deeper self without worrying about what tomorrow might bring.

Another huge benefit is that it allows you to live a more fulfilling and meaningful life while maintaining good mental health. When you work for yourself, you will set your hours and schedule, which gives you more control. It means that you can spend more time on personal relationships along with yourself, which is probably the best thing about living an independent lifestyle!

Physical Independence:

Being physically independent means that you're able to live life on your own terms. You no longer need someone else to care for you, provide for you, or accompany you when traveling. It can be a great liberation and allows you more freedom for your social development.

Financial Independence:

Living financially independent is one of the much-needed benefits of living independently. When you are dependent on others, your finances are always at their mercy, and they have the power to control you. It means you are dependent on financial support. When you live independently, your money is yours! You can save it, spend it wisely, and invest it however you want, and you no longer have to live in fear of financial ruin.

Social Independence:

Being socially independent means not depending on other people for companionship or friendship. When you live independently, it's easy to find friends and socialize without having to worry about anyone imposing their agenda. You can join clubs or organizations that interest you or just wander around town alone and enjoy the company of your thoughts.

Emotional/Mental Independence:

When you're emotionally independent, you no longer rely on others for your feelings. You don't need someone else to validate or tell you that you're okay. Instead, you learn how to deal with your emotions on your own accord and develop a strong sense of self-confidence.

It allows you to be more assertive and take control of your life. It can be a massive advantage for your intellectual growth and creativity. Also, you learn to take charge of your mind and explore new ideas without fear of judgment.

So, which one of these have you secured already?

- Physical Independence
- Financial Independence
- Social Independence
- Emotional/Mental Independence

I am sure that you did not tick every point. It takes time. If you have, maintain it. If not, there is nothing to worry about. You can now start preparing yourself and secure your independence. **Remember**, never take illegal routes to obtain your independence - I condemn that.

Becoming independent

If you have one or many box(es) unchecked or if you are not confident of your response. The below statements must help you understand what you can start working on.

BEING INDEPENDENT

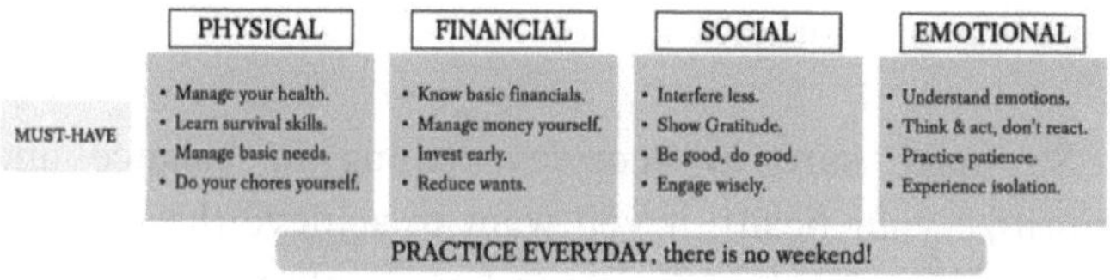

Figure 7.0 - Being Independent Must-Haves

Once you have mastered the must-haves, there is no stopping you. You will start to see the below changes in your life.

1. You have more control over your decisions.

2. You have more flexibility and improved time management skills.

3. You're able to save money.

4. You can focus on what's important.

Importance of health

Choosing to stay independent is fantastic, but you must also stay healthy. There is no discounting here. A baseline of happy and peaceful independence is good health. Healthy eating habits, regular exercise, and a good night's sleep are all essential for maintaining a healthy body. If you neglect any of these areas, you will hinder your independence in some way or another.

So make sure to keep everything in balance and prioritize your health if you want to achieve the ultimate goal. It is possible by following a few simple guidelines:

1. **Eat nutrient-rich foods** - This is one of the best ways to live without dependency. These foods will help you stay energized and focused throughout the day. They will also give you the vitamins, minerals, and antioxidants to stay healthy overall. For this, you don't spend a lot of money buying superfoods. Stay within your reach and explore the alternatives. There are many.

2. **Get adequate exercise** - Exercise is another proven way to stay healthy and independent. It not only helps to keep your body fit, but it can also improve your mood and concentration. You don't have to spend money to stay fit. Follow the simple formula - Eat less, move more. That's it.

3. **Make sure to get enough sleep** - A good night's sleep is essential for staying healthy and independent. Living tired can lead to mistakes and poor decision-making, which leads to dependency on others. Make sure to get at least 7 hours of sleep every night!

4. **Live a stress-free lifestyle** - One of the contributors to dependency is stress. Stressing out makes it hard to think straight or make good decisions. To avoid trying to live a stress-free lifestyle as much as possible by negating negative thoughts and keeping your focus on what's important (you!).

We all love gossip, be it political, entertainment, or related to family and friends. If the conversation is not fruitful for your purpose, then you must not stay there. Keep moving.

There are many ways of living a healthy lifestyle that can help you avoid dependency, so be sure to take advantage of them!

In my observation, low-income families are healthier than the rest. It is a direct relation that you don't need money to stay healthy. It is a choice. So, if you ever get a chance, ensure you learn from them.

Independent social life

There's a reason why people traditionally associate independence with adulthood: it's an important milestone in our development. As we grow older, we increasingly want to be self-sufficient and do things on our terms.

Though it may take some time, eventually most of us reach the point where we want to build a social life. It is especially true if we're dissatisfied with the limited social circles that we're stuck in. For someone independent, you'll see that they keep their social interactions to a minimum.

The best way to build a social life while living alone depends on your interests, lifestyle, and personality. However, here are some things that you may want to look at:

1. **Join online communities** - Many online communities are available to people who live an independent lifestyle. By joining these communities, you'll be able to connect with like-minded individuals and explore the various opportunities and activities that are available for you.

2. **Attend meet-ups and events** - If you're interested in meeting new people and getting involved in different activities, try attending meet-ups and events. That will not only allow you to socialize but also to learn about new opportunities and trends.

3. **Connect with friends offline** - One of the benefits of living an independent life is the freedom to do what you

want when you want. That means that you can connect with friends offline as well as online. If socializing isn't your thing, there's no reason why you can't just enjoy a glass of wine or a good book together!

It depends on your definition of "social life." If you're looking for friends with whom you can share activities and hobbies, it's probably not the best idea for you to live independently. However, if you're looking for a more passive form of socializing - where you occasionally catch up over coffee or a quick meal, independent living is the perfect solution.

Ultimately, the best way to figure out if independent living is right for you is to take a step back and evaluate what you're looking for in social life. Once you have a better sense of that, you will make the necessary adjustments in your lifestyle.

Support system for Independent life

Building a sustainable support system is incredibly helpful when living an independent life. Not only will it allow you to lean on others when you need it, but it can also give you a sense of community and belonging. A support system is also known as a "support net." Life is dynamic, and you don't know when a change will upset your setup. It is always wise to have a support system to fall back.

There are many ways you can build your support system. You could try joining local groups or organizations focusing on independent living or reach out to friends and family members who live on their own. In addition, it's always helpful to have an emergency contact person - someone you can call when the chips are down - and you need help getting through something rough.

Here are some tips to help you build a supportive network:

1. **Join a support group** - There are several support groups available online, or you can search for local groups near you. Joining a group will provide emotional support and allow you to share your experiences and get advice from others who have gone through the same things.

2. **Connect with friends and family** - One of the best ways to build a supportive network is by connecting with your loved ones. Whether through social media, email, or face-to-face conversations, spending time with loved ones helps to build strong connections.

3. **Volunteer and donate time** - Another great way to connect with others and build community is by volunteering and donating your time to worthwhile causes. Not only will this give you a sense of satisfaction, but it will also lead to finding new friends who share your values.

Maintaining White Space

Everyone needs space to reflect and to be themselves. You need your "me" time too. Am I right? It promotes self-reliance and is incredibly rewarding. It allows you to focus on your interests and priorities, and it helps you to recharge for the next day. More importantly, having time for yourself lets you enjoy your hobbies and activities without feeling pressured or obligated to do anything else.

It is essential for developing strong self-esteem. Spending time alone thinking about your thoughts and feelings helps you to reflect on who you are and what makes you unique. This process builds confidence in you.

So, define your "minimum dependency" and block some time each week for you. Make sure it's a regular habit, not just something that happens once on a full moon. Over time, this will help create healthier relationships with others and promote your independent lifestyle.

Positive growth when you live independently

Your brain grows in many ways. One of the most important things your mind does when you live independently is tuning its ability to solve problems. That is because you will not rely on someone else to do it for you. It allows your mind to become more creative and efficient in problem-solving.

Another thing your brain does when you live independently is grow its ability to think outside the box. That is because you will think outside of your normal boundaries that are set for you by society. It allows you to come up with new and innovative ideas that may not have been possible if you lived in a traditional setting.

So, if you're curious about the world of independent living and want to know what it's like, many resources can help. Independent life is a great way to explore new opportunities and gain unique skills, so don't hesitate to explore them!

The role of willpower

Without willpower, nothing is possible. If you have survived till today, that means you have the willpower. All you need to do is strengthen it further. Your willpower is the engine that propels you forward in your life. It gets you out of bed daily and pushes you to achieve your goals. To reach your full potential, having strong willpower is key. And there are several ways that you can strengthen it:

1) **Be persistent** - Nothing worth achieving comes easy. It includes becoming stronger willpower creatures. You need to be patient with yourself, even if the process is slow. Over time, however, results will start showing up.

2) **Be positive** – Seeing the world in a positive light is one of the most powerful ways to strengthen your willpower. When you approach life with a sense of optimism, it becomes much harder to give up on your goals. Consequently, this can lead to greater success down the line.

3) **Stay focused** – It's easy to get sidetracked when trying to build willpower muscle - when temptations appear in your environment constantly. To stay on track, make sure that you set clear and concise goals for yourself and stick to them until you achieve them.

So, how do you increase your willpower?

First and foremost, minimize the amount of time you spend on negative thoughts. That means you must resist the temptation to think about things that make you sad, terrified, or angry and instead focus on positive things.

Next, establish healthy boundaries with people and activities. That means defining clear parameters for when and how you conduct relationships. It also involves setting realistic expectations where you do not get pushed into situations too difficult or overwhelming.

Finally, it's important to take care of yourself emotionally and mentally by nourishing your mind and body with nutritious foods and adequate rest.

Activity 1:

Okay, let us now find your willpower by playing the itch game.

Wherever you are, you might have the urge to itch your body. It may be your thighs, ears, nose, eyes, beard, head, fingers, or arms. It may be any part of your body.

All you need to do is DON'T itch.

The idea is to check how long you can resist itching. The best part is if you itch or don't itch, the feeling of itching eventually subsides. So, there is nothing to worry about. Go ahead and use the below space. Note down your time as to how long you resisted the temptation of itching.

ITCH RESISTANCE TABLE - WORKSHEET

RECORD YOUR RESULTS

#	PLACE OF ITCH	RESISTED TIME (mm:ss)	OUTCOME
1			
2			
3			
4			
5			

Activity 1: Itch Resistance Table - Record your results.

Apply this methodology to other temptations or pain that you have. Eventually, you will win this game. The more you resist the temptation, the more you increase your levels of willpower. Play this with your peers, family, kids, and friends. Check who's willpower is strong.

Using the same method, you can test other temptations like eating habits, smoking, drinking, pain, workouts, and waking up in the morning. Create a table of your own and track your willpower graph.

Oh boy! While writing this, I wanted to itch my back, lips, head, nose, and arms. It was crazy. Check out my results below.

ITCH RESISTANCE TABLE

KRISHNA RESULTS

#	PLACE OF ITCH	RESISTED TIME (mm:ss)	OUTCOME
1	Back	00:21	Itched
2	Lips	00:44	Subsided
3	Head	00:27	Subsided
4	Nose	00:12	Itched
5	Arms	00:31	Subsided

Figure 7.1 - Sample results for Itch Resistance

Willpower is an essential tool for any successful person. It's the ability to focus on what you want and ensure you reach your goals. Remember, with enough willpower, anything is possible!

Need versus Want: How should you balance this?

The theory of need versus want is a psychological theory that helps to balance our lives. It is the natural tendency to want what they lack and avoid what they perceive as a threat. This theory can help us to make better decisions by letting us identify our needs and curb our impulses.

For example, let's say you are anxious about a job interview you will attend later that day. Your 'need' would be to get ready for the interview and feel confident, while you would 'want' not to think about the interview at all. Understanding your 'needs' and regulating your 'wants' can help you better manage your anxiety and create a more balanced life.

Another example is that let's say you saw a new advertisement for a smartphone. You would 'want' to have one, while your 'need' would be to stay with what you already have if it serves the purpose of communication. By understanding and acknowledging your needs - you can make better decisions about what is important to you.

When you find a balance between need and want, it reduces the stress that accompanies trying to meet all of your goals at once. It also allows you to make more informed decisions about what is truly important to you and how you can best achieve those goals.

Activity 2:

NEEDS-WANTS TABLE - WORKSHEET

MAKE A LIST

#	YOUR NEEDS	YOUR WANTS
1		
2		
3		
4		
5		

Activity 2: List your needs and wants

Minimalistic living approach

Have you ever wondered how many things surrounding you add value to your purpose? Look around and evaluate. Minimalistic living is a way of life that focuses on minimalism and getting the most out of what you have. It's all about living with as few possessions as possible while enjoying your life.

As young people, there are several different ways to go about minimalist living, but the goal is always the same: to live in a way that is both comfortable and efficient. The approach will vary depending on your lifestyle and needs.

1. Decide what you need - Minimalistic living doesn't mean living without anything - it just means being selective about what you bring into your life. That can be a challenging habit, but it will become easier.

2. Spend less and invest more - Yes, all the experts in this field say, spend less and invest more. That means investing your money instead of spending it on unnecessary things. It can be difficult at first, but with practice, it will become your second nature.

3. Simplify your life - One of the best ways to simplify your life is by decluttering and organizing your home and study area. All the clutter around you is a distraction - minimize it.

4. Live simple - Reduce your addiction to unhealthy habits and start eating healthy foods, get enough exercise, and enjoy simple pleasures like reading books or walking in nature. It will calm your mind and aid you in thinking better.

BEING MINIMALIST - WORKSHEET

MAKE A LIST

#	WHAT DO YOU WISH TO REMOVE?
1	
2	
3	
4	
5	

Activity 3: List your possessions that you wish to declutter

Revisit this list and see how you have progressed in a few months.

CHAPTER EIGHT

FAILING HAPPILY

Failure + Happiness ➔ Incredible Learnings

It is frustrating, annoying, and disheartening when you fail. You will feel like you're not good enough or don't deserve success. You will even feel like giving up on your goals. I did. I have failed so many times that I have lost count.

During my school days, I also practiced a classical form of dance, Bharatanatyam. It was on the occasion of Ganesh Chaturthi (symbolizing new beginnings and negating obstacles). My Guru, Smt. Jyothi Pattabhiram organized an event for her students to perform in front of an audience. Her dream was to introduce her students to the community as performers and to build their confidence. It was my first solo appearance.

For this special occasion, she composed a new choreography for me, Jatiswaram. Jatiswaram is all about rhythmic patterns without poetry. It helps master the art of stability while enlightening the performer and entertaining the observer. We spent many days practicing the moves and making corrections along the way. She believed in me.

On the day of the performance, the stage gleamed with decorations. The community audience of 200-300 people sat comfortably, waiting for us to perform. It all started well, but a few minutes into the performance, my memory failed me - I went blank. I forgot all the moves and sequences and started to panic.

It was a live concert with musicians who assisted my act. At that moment, I abruptly stopped and stood still while I covered my face with shame. Literally! I tried recalling the moves for a few seconds but failed miserably. The panic rose exponentially, and I ran back to the dressing room without completing the performance.

Uff! That was my first big failure in performance arts. While I was in the dressing room and my friends tried to console me, my Guru took to the stage and said one thing. "Look, even Mahatma Gandhi failed in his first appearance in court as a lawyer. So do not worry, take this as a lesson and move on". It wasn't easy for me then. It took years to recover from this failure. But eventually, I realized that if I hadn't failed then - I would have never gained the confidence I have today.

So, that was my first instance of a failure that bumped me to the rocks.

But now, I firmly believe that failing is part of the learning process. It's important to remember that failure isn't a bad thing. It's just another step on the road to success. The key is to take each failure as an opportunity to learn and improve. You can then use these lessons to build a foundation for future success. It's important to stay positive and motivated throughout your journey. When things get tough, silence your mind in isolation and find a way to refocus and switch gears – this will help you keep moving forward toward your goals.

Failing allows you to improve and become better at whatever you're trying to do. Once you have learned your lesson from failure, there is no need to dwell on it further. Let them go as soon as possible and move on with your life. Remember, they're just lessons that will help you become a better person in the future.

Tell me one thing. You don't think about the subject you failed at school when you were little, right? You have moved on. So, apply the same method and keep doing it.

Why do you fail?

Your mind is tuned to keep learning. And learning can progress only when you fail. The first time you attempt an activity, you might not put in the hard work or may not have followed the process and made a critical mistake. That is a failure and is inevitable - no one succeeds without some level of defeat along the journey. Once you accept this fact, it becomes much easier to start moving forward and learning from your failures. Some common reasons why you fail,

- You don't have the ability.
- You don't take action.
- You don't set goals and deadlines.
- You don't measure your progress.
- You don't hold yourself accountable.
- You're not persistent enough.

Make sure that you understand what factor led to your previous failure. That will help you avoid repeating the same mistakes and identify potential solutions to problems. It's what makes us stronger and more motivated to try again. If you're willing to take the risk and push yourself beyond your comfort zone, you're sure to succeed in the end.

Temporary nature of the failure

Yes, like everything else, failure is also temporary. How often have you heard someone say, "failure is the best teacher"? Failure teaches us a lot about ourselves. It forces us to introspect and figure out why we failed. We learn what our weaknesses are and how to work around them.

Failure also teaches us how to overcome adversity. When things get tough, we remember how we overcame our failures in the past and use those same strategies when faced with similar challenges in the future. The more experience you have with defeat, the better your chances of success. One thing to keep in mind is that everyone fails at something from time to time. What really counts is how you respond to failure and what lessons you learn from it.

Understand that,

- Failure is inevitable.
- Failure is a sign of progress.
- Failure is a stepping stone to success.

Just because something fails once doesn't mean you will always fail in the future. In fact, failing leads to success because it forces you to reevaluate your goals and strategies to find a better way forward. This process can help you develop and understand yourself and your business.

Remember! Remember! Remember!

Like failure, success is also temporary. Your humility is what makes you stand out. That is what drives you closer to your purpose. Treat success and failure the same way. Don't be afraid to fail, and don't forget your humility when you succeed. If you fulfill your purpose, it is time to upgrade your goal to the next level.

Now pause for a moment and read the above statement once more. If required, highlight the paragraph so you can return to it again.

The joy of failing happily

How many times have you smiled when you failed? Very few, correct? But why? Have you ever asked yourself? That is the difference. When you have realized the importance of failure, you will never crib or cry when you fail. Instead, you will smile and be happy.

For one thing, you might be thinking of the consequences of failure, right? Thinking of all those will not give you any satisfaction. So, move on. Take the learning and be better next time.

Only when we fail do we realize what lies ahead. And that strengthens our resolve to achieve our goals. Failure teaches us to be resilient, persistent, realistic and focused. In fact, if you make it a habit of failing – even in small increments – your innate creativity will kick in and lead you forward towards success.

Failures force us to face our shortcomings head-on. That's what makes it so pleasurable - we know that we're not alone in our struggles and that there are people out there who have gone through similar things before us.

So whether you're fighting an uphill battle or just starting your journey, remember to embrace failure wholeheartedly - it will make your path much more enjoyable overall.

There is no reason for you to frown. Stay happy when you fail.

1. **Failing can** help you learn new skills and strategies. As you go through the process of failing, you'll likely learn something new that will help you in your future endeavors.

2. **Failing can** make you more resilient. When things get tough, failing can make you stronger. It will force you to face the challenges and figure out how to solve them.

3. **Failing can** lead to success. The more times you fail, the better opportunities you'll have for success the next time around. You'll know what it takes to succeed and be able to apply those same skills when the opportunity arises.

The key to a happy failure is accepting that you will make mistakes and learn from them as quickly as possible. This way, you won't waste any time or energy feeling miserable about your mistakes - instead, you will focus on moving forward.

And who knows? - Maybe one day your success will be based on a mistake you made happily!

The modulation rule

By now, you must have understood the nature of failure and success. They are not permanent states. Nothing is. So it makes sense for us to apply the modulation rule.

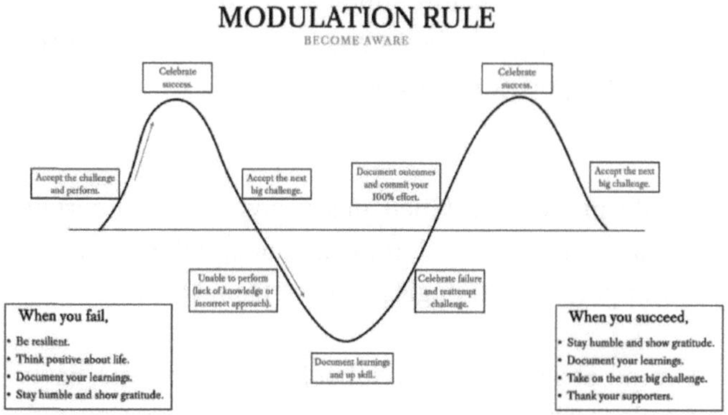

Figure 8.0 - Modulation Rule

3-point perspective toward failure

- **Failure is not** the end of the world - just like anything else in life, failure is a learning experience that leads to success. Remember, it's never too late to start over and try again!

- **Failure is not** a reflection of your character - everyone around you experiences failure in many ways, and it doesn't reflect on your virtue as a person. You are not alone - some people have also faced failure and managed to come out stronger.

- **Failure is not** a sign that you're not good enough - on the contrary, failure indicates that you're doing something right. It shows you what you need to work on and helps you grow as a person.

While many have failed miserably and have certainly shown us how to succeed, they have adapted to the failures and built personal strategies to learn from them.

For me, at a personal level. Look at your parents, haven't they failed? They may have had different parenting styles, but they all faced defeat back then, shaping them into what they are today. They are now successful individuals. Isn't it?

It is important not to be afraid to fail but look at it as an opportunity for personal growth and development. Take all the constructive feedback and focus on leaving your insecurities behind. Your parents are the best role models that you can have.

Let's also consider '**you.**' You have also failed numerous times and have stood firm to try again with a positive mindset. You have studied and learned from your failures. You are not afraid to take on new challenges. And you are grateful for the experiences that have led you to where you are today.

One piece of advice is to be fearless. The fear of failure will take you nowhere. Fearlessness can help you take risks and try new things, complementing greater success. This trait is crucial to succeeding in anything, be it a business venture, creative project, or relationship. If you are fearless, you will take on any challenge and emerge victorious.

If you're looking for a world without failures, you're in for a difficult journey. Without it, there would be no opportunity for learning and growth. Failure is one of the best things that can happen to you because it teaches you how to cope with setbacks and handle stress. It will teach you the art of perseverance. Every failure leads to new opportunities, new learning, subject matter expertise, and new ideas.

It boosts your self-confidence. So be brave and keep moving forward. The only highway for success is the one that leads to continued failure. So keep trying, even when you think things are going wrong. Keep learning from your mistakes, and you'll soon find that rhythm where failure becomes happiness and happiness becomes a success.

CHAPTER NINE

DETACHMENT

Attachment (⬇) ➔ Peace (⬆)

From birth, you attach to things and feelings. It all starts with toys, tricycles, and anyone who offers you food. As you grow up to teens, you start attaching yourself to cycles, bikes, flowers, animals, and people. During your life, you will encounter many different things that make you feel good or bad, loved or hated. You'll attach yourself to these experiences to create a sense of who you are.

It is human nature to attach yourself to things. There are several reasons why you do this. One reason is that it provides a sense of security. When you attach yourself to something, you know it's there for you no matter what happens. It gives you a sense of stability and reassurance, which is very comforting. Isn't it?

Another reason you attach yourself to things is it makes you feel good. It makes you feel like you're in charge – like you're in control of your life. This feeling of control gives you peace and self-confidence, which is very helpful when times are tough.

However, it's important not to get too caught up in your attachments as they can ultimately be destructive. Depending on someone or something else for happiness, security, or self-esteem, you become disappointed and disillusioned. All your attachments will then serve only to make your life difficult instead of easier.

When you're attached to something or someone, it's hard to think objectively about them. You tend to see only the good qualities, which makes it tough to deal with them firmly or impartially. As a result, you react emotionally instead of rationally when things go wrong.

Importance of Detachment

For ages, our sages have preached and practiced detachment. It has led many people to experience joy when practiced diligently. You start to see life from a detached perspective, allowing you to make better decisions and be happier overall. It's all about being in the present moment and not letting your emotions get in the way of your logical thinking. It also allows you to be transparent with yourself, which is essential for maintaining a healthy ego and emotional balance in difficult situations.

Being detached lets you set your own standards instead of feeling proud, self-conscious, or embarrassed. When you disengage yourself from emotions, you're free to live life more fully and enjoy the moment.

Another benefit of detachment is that it can help reduce stress levels. When stressed out, your brain releases chemicals like adrenaline making it harder to think straight. Detachment will calm you down, and you will make more accurate decisions under pressure.

It can be quite liberating when it happens naturally instead of being forced upon you by other people or circumstances. You learn to let go of things that don't serve you while helping you find true happiness and peace. Detachment is controlling your emotions and feelings to live life without them constantly interfering with your ability to think clearly and act rationally.

It is a key component of mindfulness, and it's something that can be difficult to learn. But, by practicing detachment, you can gradually free yourself from the adverse effects of your past experiences and create a more positive future.

Unlocking happiness

When you detach, it helps you be more objective and unbiased when dealing with any situation. That can lead to a better understanding of things with increased clarity. It allows you to make sound judgments and take action accordingly, which is beneficial in all areas of your life.

Also, it enables you to be more flexible and open-minded. When detached emotionally, it's easier for you to accept different perspectives and insights without getting attached to either side. And you reach new conclusions and find solutions that work best for everyone involved.

Detachment makes it easier for you to focus on the things that are important to you. When your emotions are preoccupied with negative or toxic thoughts, it becomes difficult for you to think straight or get anything done. Detachment helps you be clear and focused on the things that really matter, which is why it's such a valuable life skill.

It is a key component of happiness, and it's something that you can learn to achieve through practice.

Repeat the below statements in your mind at least **FIVE** times a day.

- I have emotions and feelings - I will not let them control me.
- I understand my emotions and feelings - I know what they are.
- I will remain objective and unbiased in all of my dealings.
- My happiness is not dependent on the opinion or reaction of others.
- I am flexible and open-minded, and I will accept different perspectives and insights.

Improved Relationships when Detached

When you're detached, it's easier to maintain healthy relationships. You won't be as reactive or upset when things don't go your way. And you'll better understand how other people think and feel. That makes communication much smoother, which leads to stronger ties between you and those around you.

In addition, detachment allows you to set boundaries more easily. When your emotions are out of control, it's often difficult to identify what's appropriate and what's not. With detachment, however, this becomes less of an issue. Because you understand that you don't need to control or be controlled by your emotions.

Do you know that a well-managed detachment makes it easier for you to categorize your activities in life? It means that you can separate your relationship from work or any other activities - giving you more control and intensifying the process towards success.

It will also help you develop a more positive attitude. When your emotions get caught up in negative thoughts and memories, it's hard to be cheerful or optimistic. However, with practice, you can learn to detach yourself from these things and maintain a more positive outlook on life. So, detachment is something that you can learn to achieve through practice. If you're able to do this regularly, it will impact positively on your overall well-being.

Here is what you will gain,

- You will not worry as much as you do now.
- You will start forgiving.
- Your productivity and creativity will get a boost.
- You will experience peace of mind.
- You will receive better love.

Takeaways:

1. Detachment is vital in maintaining healthy relationships.
2. When your emotions are under control, it's easier to communicate and build stronger ties with others.
3. Detaching yourself from negative thoughts and memories helps develop a positive attitude towards life.
4. Practice is key to mastering detachment.

My secret tradition

Like everything else, detachment is also a skill you can learn over time. You know how to tie your shoelace and how to eat, correct? That is because you mastered it for a long time. If you want to detach yourself from being over-attached to your emotions, practice doing it regularly.

Follow the 4 box evaluation mentioned below.

4 BOX EVALUATION

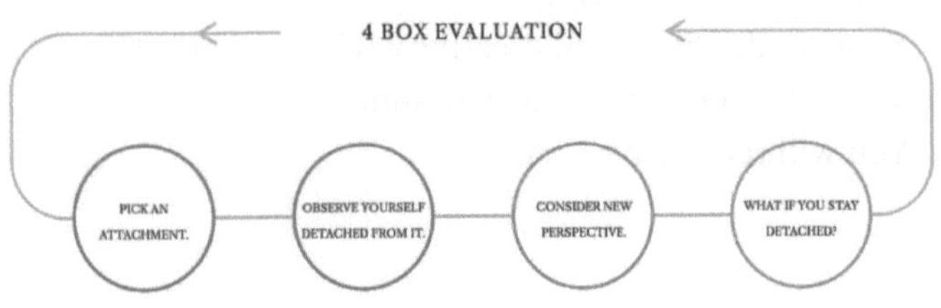

Figure 9.0 - Four Box Evaluation Method for any attachment

I use this method of evaluation as a tradition. There is no escape from encountering the attachments in life. They keep bombarding us more often. Whenever my mind meets a new attachment, I evaluate them. Try it yourself and document your thoughts.

Activity 1:

Think of an attachment:

Pick something that you are attached to and mull over it to vegetate.

4 BOX EVALUATION - WORKSHEET

ATTACHMENT IDENTIFICATION

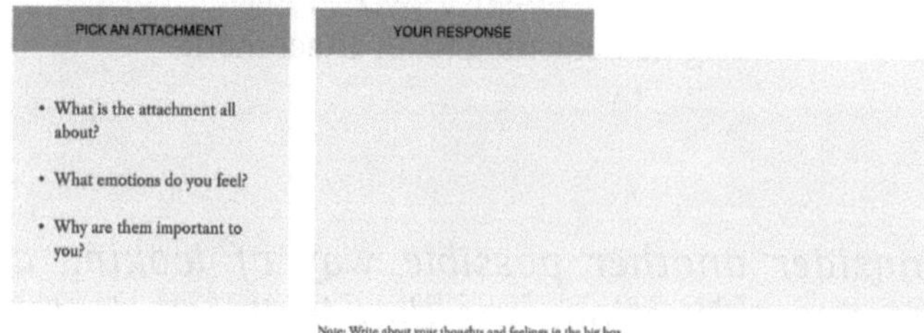
PICK AN ATTACHMENT

- What is the attachment all about?
- What emotions do you feel?
- Why are them important to you?

YOUR RESPONSE

Note: Write about your thoughts and feelings in the big box.

Activity 1.0: Document your response to an attachment

Observe yourself detached from the attachment.

4 BOX EVALUATION - WORKSHEET

ATTACHMENT DETACHMENT

OBSERVE YOURSELF DETACHED FROM IT.	YOUR RESPONSE
• How does it make you feel now? • Is it less important than before? • Write a possible reason why that may be so.	

Note: Write about your thoughts and feelings in the big box.

Activity 1.1: Document your response when you imagine detaching to an attachment

Consider another possible way of looking at the same situation, one that isn't attached to emotions.

4 BOX EVALUATION - WORKSHEET

NEW PERSPECTIVE OF ATTACHMENT

CONSIDER NEW PERSPECTIVE.	YOUR RESPONSE
• What is the reason for this attachment? • What are the facts attached to it? • Is this attachment valuable to my purpose?	

Note: Write about your thoughts and feelings in the big box.

Activity 1.2: Document your response when you consider a new perspective

What do you think would happen if you continued to detach yourself from the attachment?

4 BOX EVALUATION - WORKSHEET

WHAT-IF

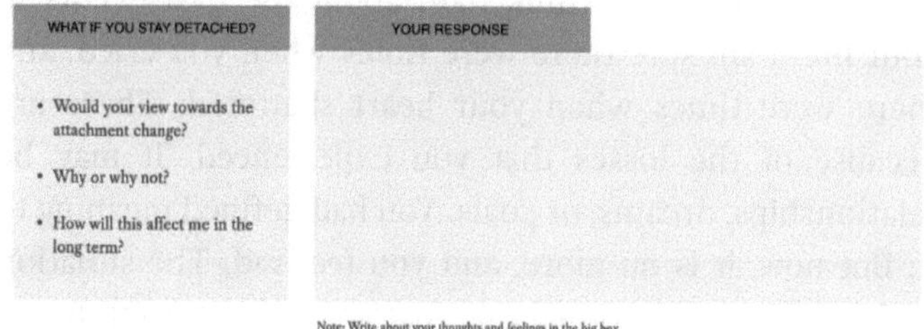

Activity 1.3: Document your response when you stay detached

If you'd like, write about any other thoughts that come to your mind.

Keep the below points in mind:

- Evaluate your perspective on it.
- Validate your actions.
- Make harmless but advantageous decisions.
- Implement slowly.

Let Go

Take a moment and think hard about the past events in your life. I am sure there were times when you cried, and there were times when your heart shattered. These are because of the losses that you experienced. It may be relationships, dreams, or goals. You had defined meaning to it. But now, it is no more, and you feel sad. The situation took you on an emotional ride that you did not want. But at the back of your mind, you still think about it. You still cry and experience that pain. Why?

In the same way, think of all your successes. You feel happy, energized, and pumped up whenever you taste success. It is because you achieved the targets that you had set for yourself. You experienced a sense of being superior. You felt that notion of accomplishment. It may be love, securing a rank in school, winning a game, or even getting promoted at work. Again, you were highly emotional. These feelings rest in your mind forever. And, I am sure you recall them often to relive that happy moment.

I ask, why?

Why is there a need to recall our memories, happy or sad? Why should we relive them?

You may argue that it gives you strength and reminds you of your learning. There you go. In a nutshell, your memories are anchors that keep you attached to the past. They validate your decisions and help you remember those lessons you have learned in life. But at what cost? Once you have learned a lesson, more often you don't forget. There is no need to remember the entire episode of emotions. Instead, pick the learning and move on.

If you don't, your emotions take over, and you become a prisoner of your own mind. You no longer have control over yourself or the situation around you because all you can focus on is that memory that has caused pain or given momentary happiness in the past. You have to fight hard not to let it control you.

So the next time you are emotional about the past, ask yourself: is there a need for me to recall this memory? Am I just doing it because it makes me feel better in the present? Can I try and free myself from that emotion by looking at another perspective of living in the moment?

Consider freeing yourself from those memories and emotions. They may be anchors, but they are not necessary to your happiness in the present or future. Follow the method of the **4 box rule** and gradually let go of your past. Make sure you are honest with yourself about why you're doing this.

Clinging to materialistic things

It's an epidemic in the world. And the easiest way to damage your mental and physical health. There are many reasons why you end up endorsing materialistic life. Sometimes you may be unconsciously drawn to things that make you feel good or look good. You may also believe holding more possessions will make you happier or more secure. All of these beliefs are wrong. And, I know that you understand this fact. Yet, you cling on to it.

For people who constantly worry about their material possessions - having them around can provide a sense of security. But, if those possessions aren't providing that security, then they're only serving to add stress and anxiety to the person's life. Your thoughts consume you about your wants, which takes away your ability to enjoy the present moment.

The biggest problem with materialism is that it ultimately leads to a lack of satisfaction. You may have everything you need, but if you're not happy from the inside, everything you have isn't really worth anything at all. Instead of filling your life with things that you can't control (like material possessions), let go of what doesn't matter and focus on what does: your happiness and well-being.

Activity 2:

Use the below space to list down your materialistic possessions.

MATERIALISTIC TABLE - WORKSHEET

MAKE A LIST

#	ARTICLE / ITEM	I NEED	I CAN LET GO
1			
2			
3			
4			
5			

Note: Use tick (✔) to indicate your preference.

Activity 2: Materialistic Table

If you are letting go of your possessions, here are some tips to get you started,

- Start with one thing at a time.
- Write down your thoughts and feelings.

- Be honest with yourself.

Remember that detachment doesn't mean abandoning everything and everyone that has ever mattered to you in your life. It means understanding and accepting that those things no longer have significance in your life now or in the future. Be wise and make sure your decision is on sound reasoning.

Like Simone Weil said, "*Attachment is the great fabricator of illusions; reality can be obtained only by someone who is detached.*"

CHAPTER TEN

Combination Mindset

Combination Mindset + Consistency ➔ Definite success

If eating the right food and regularly exercising keeps your body fit, having the right mindset keeps your mind healthy and fresh. Your mind is the reason for what you are. And the way you think can determine the quality of your life.

When you have a growth mindset that benefits you and the people around you, it means you are looking at life with a positive perspective. You start taking action as per your beliefs, and your objectives will have clarity. You also nurture an optimistic attitude. You believe in yourself and what you are capable of. A healthy mind is a must and can help you achieve anything.

Mindset has an impact on human performance. In particular, it determines how you approach and interact with the world, affecting your ability to achieve your goals.

There are several ways that mindset affects human performance. First, it affects how you perceive yourself and the reality around you. Depending on your mindset, you start to see things in a more positive or negative light. It can impact your mood, motivation, and consequently, your ability to perform at peak levels.

Second, mindset affects how you process information. You tend to focus on the relevant aspects of information while filtering out irrelevant details. It leads to better decision-making and better outcomes.

Last but not least, the mindset has an impact on your emotions. You are motivated and focused on your goals when it is in sync. Conversely, it can lead to stress and anxiety when you have a negative fixed mindset. It hampers your performance.

Gambling External Influences

These influences come from anywhere and everywhere and often aim to harm or control you. They try to get inside your head and influence your thoughts and actions in ways you fail to comprehend or approve of. You end up being deceived.

The common threat is from social and emotional influences. Social influences come from people around you and aim to affect your thoughts, feelings, and behavior.

Emotional influences come from within yourself and change how you feel about yourself or the world around you.

External influences can have a massive impact on your mindset. They always try to alter it, to get you to do things that will benefit the person or thing influencing you. They can make you feel anxious, happy, excited, or insecure.

There's no guarantee that external influences won't negatively affect you. But there are ways to protect yourself from them with coaching. The first step is recognizing the signs and symptoms of an external influence attempt. That includes paying attention to what's going on around you and how your emotions are changing to it.

If something seems off, it probably is!

Combination Mindset

The combination mindset is a way of thinking that allows you to see things more positively. It is a perspective of viewing your problems as opportunities and your opportunities as challenges. This way of thinking leads to a more positive outlook on life because it makes you see the world as an exciting place full of possibilities.

It is like mixing the right ingredients and preparing your favorite meal. In the chapter 'Movers and Shakers,' I introduced you to the components of a combination mindset. Let us now understand them in detail.

Trust Mindset

The first component of the combination mindset is trust. A trust mindset is a state of mind in which you believe others will act in a way that benefits you. You have faith that people will do what they say they're going to do and that they won't hurt you or take advantage of you.

To have a trusting mindset, you need to trust yourself and the people around you. First, you must trust your judgment and ability to make good decisions. You also need to trust that other people are competent and honest.

Having a trusting mindset can be beneficial when making relationships work. It can lead to smoother communication and cooperation because both parties know they can rely on the other person for support. In addition, a trusting mindset can also help build strong bonds between people because it creates an atmosphere of mutual respect.

If you have had any instances in the past where you trusted someone and it turned out they hurt you. That is not the end of the road. You can learn from those experiences and form a new, more trusting relationship in the future. The below process will help you build a stronger base.

TRUST MINDSET

TRUST

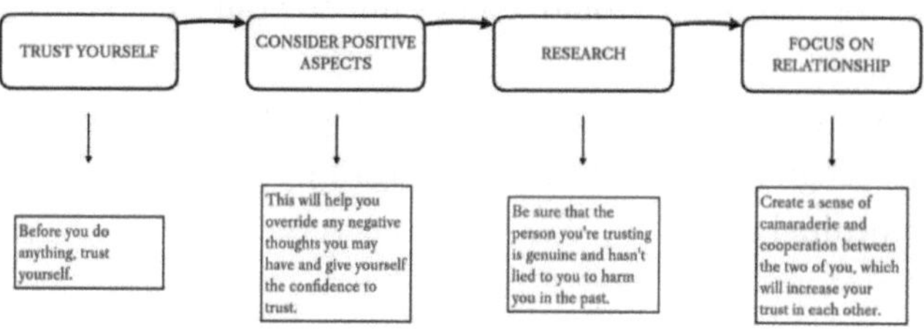

Figure 10.0 - Trust Mindset Process

Value Mindset

A value mindset is a habit of thinking about yourself and your life. It encourages you to focus on the things that are important to you. It can help you make better decisions, both big and small.

The key component of a value mindset is that you start by recognizing that everything has value. It means that anything — from your time to your skills to the things you own — has worth. When you maintain a value mindset, you know that your goals are essential. And you won't let anything stand in the way of reaching them. You're also less likely to put yourself down or feel overwhelmed by challenges.

This mindset can help you make positive decisions as well. For example, if you want to buy something, rather than focusing on what you don't have, think about the best use for that item. Would it add value to your life? **Think.**

Value comes from within – so start valuing yourself by recognizing the precious things in your life and living accordingly.

VALUE MINDSET

VALUE

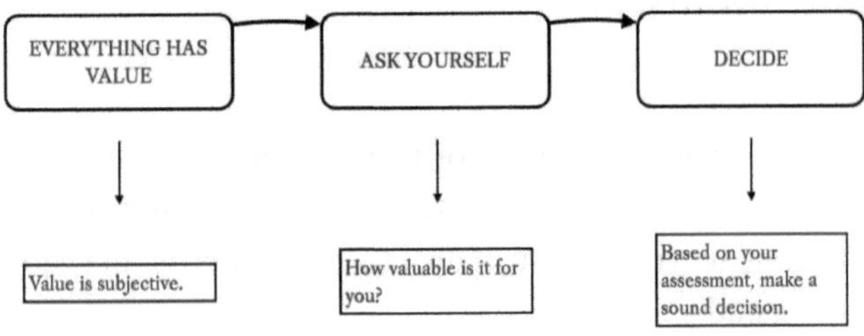

Figure 10.1 - Value Mindset Process

Courageous Mindset

A courageous mindset entails hope and optimism. It allows you to see the good in every situation, even when things seem bleak. It gives you the strength to persevere through tough times, and it enables you to face your fears.

A courageous mindset is crucial for two main reasons. Firstly, it enables you to take action. When you know that whatever you perform matters and impacts positively, the motivation to succeed is contagious.

Secondly, having a courageous mindset allows you to see the opportunity in every problem. By analyzing potential solutions rather than just problems, you are more likely to find ways to overcome them.

The best way to develop a courageous mindset is by learning from failure. Remembering what went wrong and why it can help equip you with the skills necessary for future success. Also, remember that there are always growth opportunities. Be prepared to take advantage of these opportunities, and try not to dwell on the negative aspects of life.

With a little effort, you can develop a courageous mindset that will enable you to achieve your goals no matter what obstacles stand in your way.

COURAGEOUS MINDSET

COURAGE

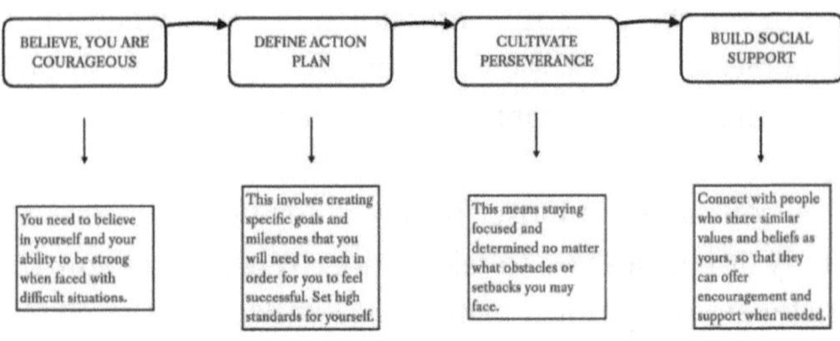

Figure 10.2 - Courageous Mindset Process

Positive Mindset

A positive mindset is a state of mind in which you are optimistic and believe that good things will happen. To maintain a positive mindset, you must keep your expectations reasonable and realistic and focus on your strengths rather than your weaknesses.

When you have a positive mindset, it will help you to be more resilient in the face of difficult situations. You'll also be less likely to give up when things get tough. It is one of the easiest mindsets to build. All you need to do is think positively and keep feeding good thoughts to your mind.

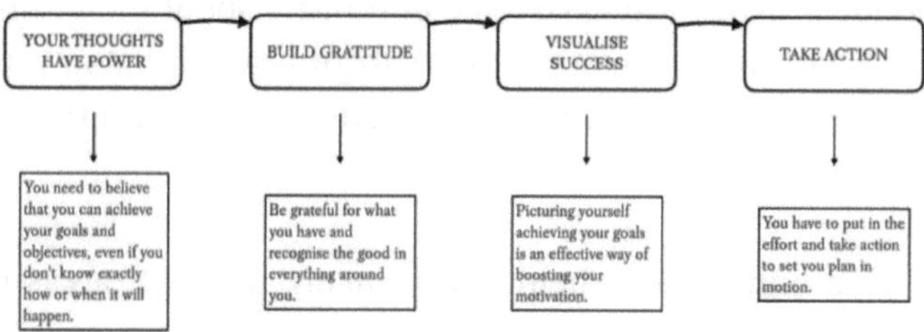

Figure 10.3 - Positive Mindset Process

Learning Mindset

A learning mindset is a type of thinking that emphasizes learning and exploration over assessment and perfectionism. When you nurture a learning mindset, you're more likely to be open to new experiences and opportunities. You'll also be less afraid of making mistakes - which is essential in any form of learning. Remember the chapter 'Failing Happily'?

A key component of having a learning mindset is knowing that progress always occurs in small increments. Rather than trying to accomplish massive goals all at once, break them down into manageable goals you can achieve over time. That will help keep you motivated and on track while giving you the sense of satisfaction that comes with consistent progress.

When it comes to learning, be open to new information and ideas. Also, you have to be optimistic about the future. Consider learning an opportunity to grow and develop your skills instead of something that needs perfect execution to be successful.

This mindset can help you in many different areas of your life. For example, if you're struggling with a task - a learning mindset will encourage you to keep trying until you succeed. It will also help you to study for exams – by focusing on the material rather than the evaluations that may come after them.

LEARNING MINDSET

NEVER STOP LEARNING

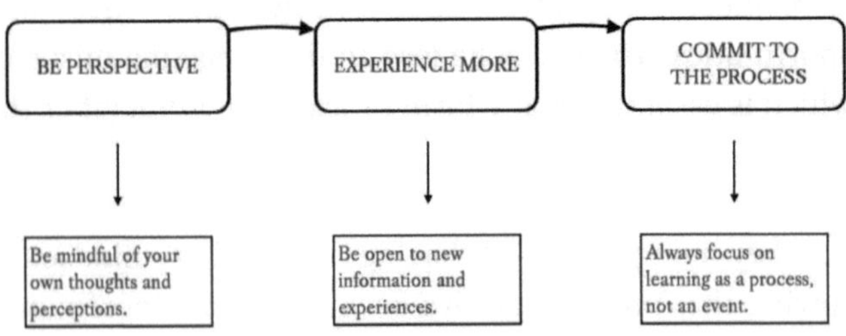

Figure 10.4 - Learning Mindset Process

Patience Mindset

When you foster a patient mindset, you'll see the positive aspects of difficult situations and remain calm. You don't get stressed out or angry. You will have the strength to handle setbacks calmly and rationally. It makes it easier for you to find solutions and reach your goals.

The key to fostering a patient mindset is knowing the emotions that affect your decisions. When you're in a stressful or difficult situation, your emotions take control and make bad choices. But if you stay aware of how you're feeling - you'll make rational decisions that will lead to success.

Patience is important. It also allows you to take time to research the options carefully before making a decision, which will help you avoid making a mistake.

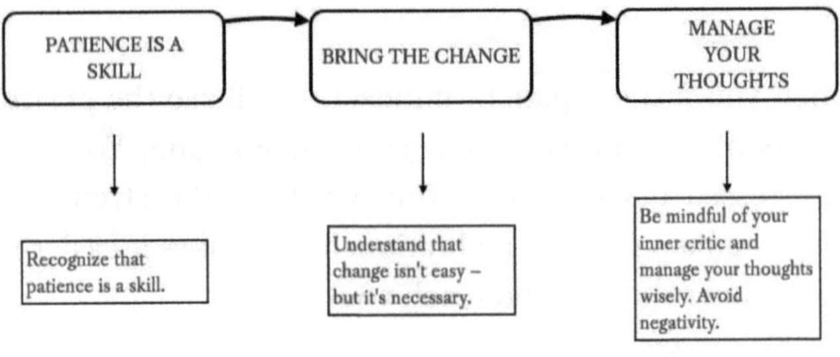

Figure 10.5 - Patience Mindset Process

Focus Mindset

A focused mindset is a practice of thinking that allows you to stay on task and accomplish what you set out to do. When you're focused, all your attention is devoted, and you concentrate entirely on what you're doing. That is how the mindset works.

With this mindset in place, you'll stay focused on your goals and objectives. You don't get sidetracked by irrelevant thoughts or distractions, meaning you can focus on the task and complete it efficiently. It also allows you to be more confident and self-reliant when solving problems, as opposed to being afraid of failure or feeling doubtful about your ability.

Having a focused mindset also helps you overcome impostor syndrome - the feeling that you don't deserve your achievements because they're not real accomplishments. Instead of getting overwhelmed by this feeling, understand that even though your work may not be recognized immediately, it's still worthwhile in the long run. And with practice and time, your work will begin to show results!

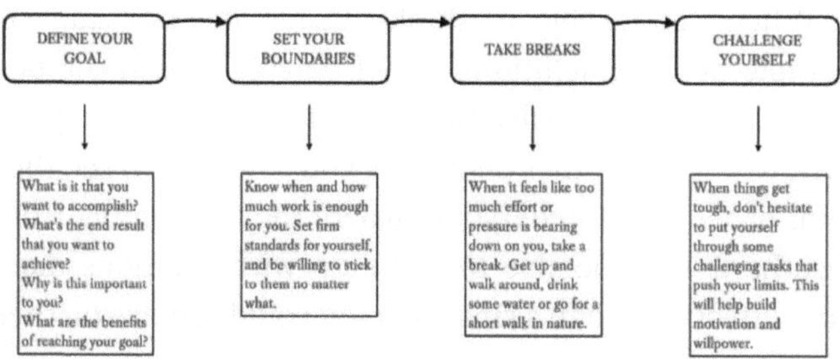

Figure 10.6 - Focus Mindset Process

Combination mindset in action

When the combination mindset is in action, wonders happen. Coming up with new ideas is no longer a challenge, as you're already in the ethos of being creative. And when it comes to completing tasks, you'll be able to do them efficiently and without feeling overwhelmed or doubtful about your ability. It allows you to be more confident and self-reliant when solving problems, leading to better success overall.

Moreover, you're now able to see the world more holistically. You'll take on multiple perspectives and look at things from many different angles. That makes it much easier to define creative solutions, as you don't get stuck in a single viewpoint.

When you're able to think outside the box and see multiple possible solutions, you'll be able to find the best one quickly. Additionally, this growth mindset can help you work better with other people, as you'll be able to see their point of view and understand where they're coming from. Together, you'll be able to come up with solutions much more effectively than a single person could achieve on their own.

The combination mindset is powerful. It will help you achieve great success in any field or activity. Implementing it will help you be more creative and efficient, see the world holistically, and work better with others. Like Carol Dweck says - "no matter what your ability is, effort is what ignites that ability and turns it into accomplishment." So if you're looking to take your success to the next level, ensure to adopt a combination mindset!

CHAPTER ELEVEN

A NOTE FROM THE AUTHOR - SMILE

Life is like a child, just like you. It will throw tantrums as frequently as possible. At the same time, it is fun if you have understood how to be with it. You have one life to live, and it offers you plenty of opportunities. It is up to you how you make the best of it. So, enjoy life to the fullest. Smile now and then.

Make the most of this life by living in the present moment and enjoying every minute. **Be proactive** in your planning and make sure that you're taking advantage of opportunities that come your way. You should also be **mindful** of your health and live a healthy lifestyle for yourself and those around you.

Keep your morale high by enjoying the little things in life – like a good book or a relaxing bath. Remember, life is full of surprises. Enjoy every moment and smile – it will put everyone around you at ease.

Many people avoid taking risks because they think they might fail. But actually, this is what allows us to grow and learn new things. When you **take calculated risks**, you're opening yourself up to new opportunities, which will help you grow as a person and creator.

Sometimes all we need is a little guidance from our inner voice not to get lost on our path back home. If something feels right or if it seems like it would be beneficial for both you and others involved, go with it!

Living life without worrying too much can be difficult, but it's possible with the right approach. Make a list of your priorities and stick to them. It will help you stay on track and avoid getting sidetracked by trivial things. Stay positive and apply self-talk that allows you to stay in a good mood. That will help you remain calm in stressful situations and resist negative impulses. I always keep saying - ***"talking to self isn't madness."***

Set reasonable expectations for yourself, and don't overcomplicate things. It will help you manage your stress better and avoid feeling overwhelmed by everything that comes your way. Take time for yourself every day, even if it's just for 10 minutes. It will help you relax, de-stress, and recharge your batteries. And you'll be ready to take on the next day's challenges.

Everyone enjoys life in different ways. It is up to you to choose what works best for you. In general, live in the present moment. Don't focus too much on the past or the future – just enjoy what's happening right now. That is how you learn from the past while creating your future.

Stay optimistic. When you're feeling down about something, it's hard to enjoy anything else. Instead, try to find something good in every situation and take things one step at a time. Permit yourself to be silly and laugh whenever you feel like it. Life is just once as far as our current reality is. So, have fun!

Connect with others not only to increase your numbers on social media. Connect for your **purpose**. Make them feel included. Do this not only with family and friends but with strangers too. You never know when you will brighten someone's day. But, it will brighten your day when you connect with a person or any other life form on a deeper level.

Smiling can be an incredibly uplifting experience. When you smile, it not only feels good on a personal level, but it will impact positively on those around you too. A genuine smile is infectious and often leads to others smiling back – creating a sense of amity and community. So why not start making the most of every moment by giving yourself some encouragement with a smile? It could just brighten your day!

Some best practices,

- Send a random email or message to one of your contacts every day. **Show gratitude** in that email/message.
- Listen to happy music. Smile when you listen and feel the happiness that comes with it!

PS: *Whenever I wake up, I smile. It is such a simple habit. It keeps me going all day, no matter what the day offers.*

Scribble Your Thoughts

Scribble Your Thoughts

Scribble Your Thoughts

Scribble Your Thoughts

Printed by Libri Plureos GmbH in Hamburg, Germany